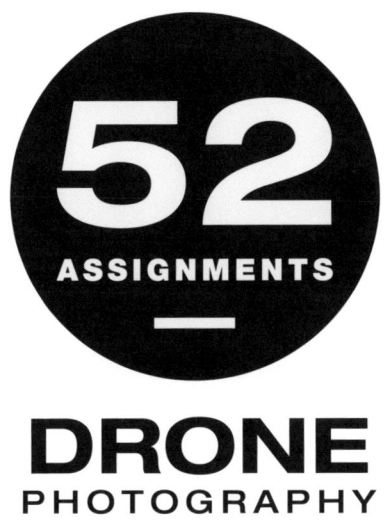

DRONE
PHOTOGRAPHY

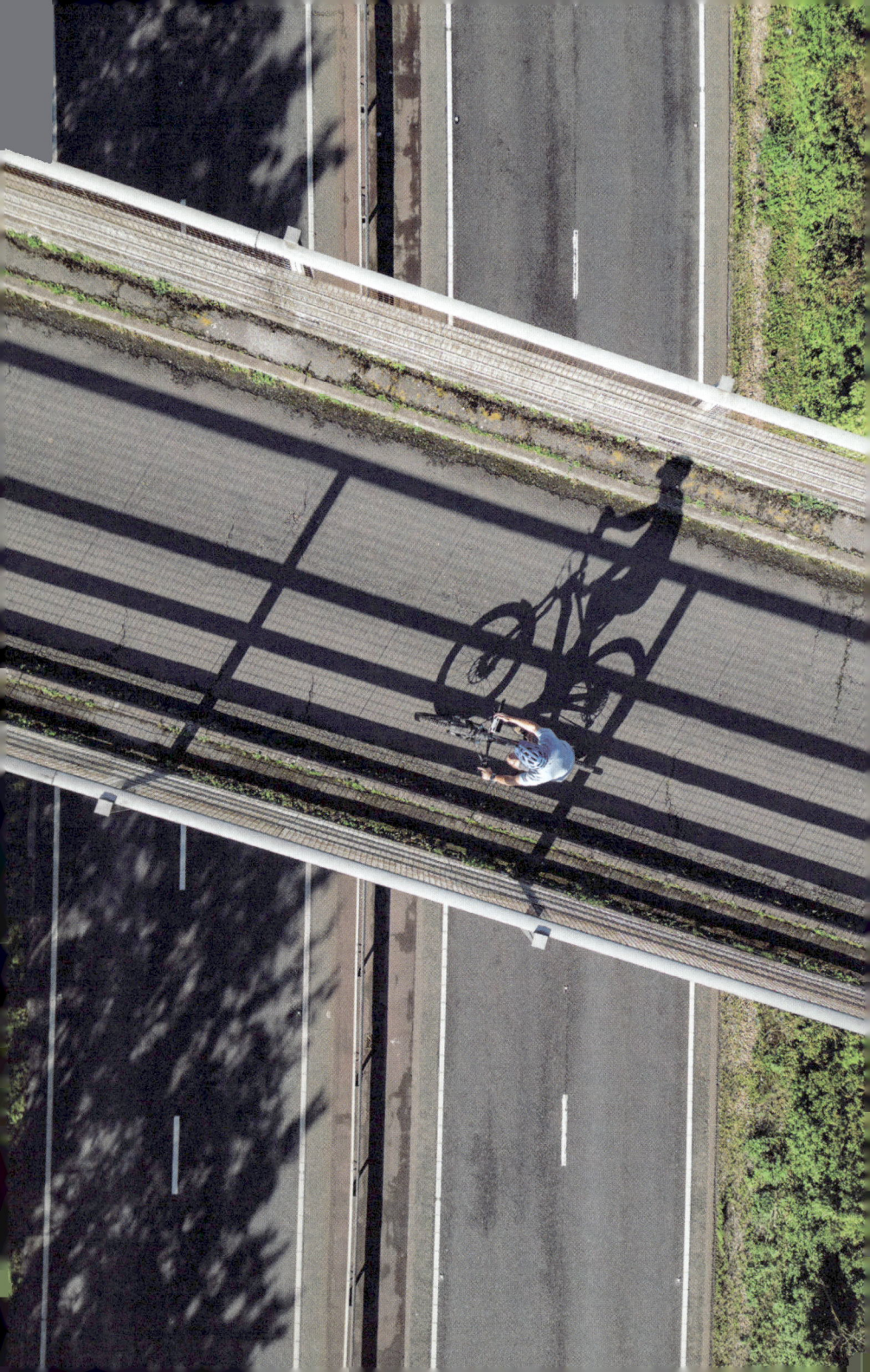

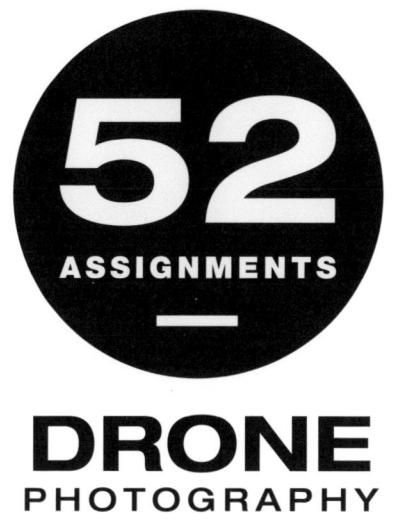

52
ASSIGNMENTS
—

DRONE
PHOTOGRAPHY

FERGUS KENNEDY

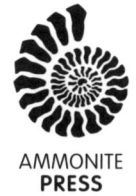

AMMONITE
PRESS

ASSIGNMENTS

Tick off your completed projects

ASSIGNMENT KEY

Each assignment has symbols showing the type of tasks involved.

 COMPUTER   CREATIVE   RESEARCH   LANDSCAPE

 EXPOSURE   VIDEO   DETAILS   ARCHITECTURE

ASSIGNMENT JOURNAL

Use the journal spaces throughout the book to keep a record of your experimental assignments and images.

_____

_____

_____

INTRODUCTION

As a photographer with my feet generally anchored firmly to the ground, the opportunity to exchange this for a bird's-eye view was once the stuff of dreams. With the advent of relatively affordable camera drones, suddenly I felt a world of new photographic possibilities opening up with all the excitement that entails.

After the initial novelty had worn off, it was sometimes difficult to find the motivation and inspiration to get the drone in the air, as I thought I might have exhausted the possibilities in my local area. To combat this creative slump, I put lots of thought into all the opportunities around me, often seeking inspiration in other forms of photography.

This book is an attempt to distill those ideas into a series of assignments that should inspire you and help answer the question, "I've bought a drone—now what?". Wherever you live, there are great drone images to be had and through these assignments you can start to explore the opportunities. Drone photography can be quite a technical undertaking, so I've tried to ensure there are assignments that will suit every skill level.

I have given you a year's worth of weekly assignments, but there is no pressure to do one every week. By working your way through the assignments, you may find that you get new ideas and go off at a tangent exploring a particularly rich seam of photographic opportunities, before returning to the assignments at a later date.

Most consumer camera drones in use today are made by one manufacturer, DJI. In this book, I have tried to be generic in my terminology wherever possible, however there are some cases where I've been more specific and used DJI terminology. If you have a non-DJI camera drone, the chances are it has similar features, although the terminology may be slightly different.

For many assignments, I encourage the use of manual camera settings; while they could be done using automatic exposure settings, using manual settings allows you to get to grips with the basics of exposure, particularly shutter speed and ISO (most consumer drones have a fixed aperture). Most assignments are stills photography, but I have included a few video-based tasks, as these can be fun and will improve your drone-flying skills, as you need to pay attention to smooth flying.

It's important to abide by the drone regulations wherever you live. You have a responsibility to be familiar with all the rules and guidelines—and be aware that often the rules are different for various weight classes of drone. Not only this, but even when flying within the rules, always be mindful of people's right to privacy and be aware of the disturbance caused by the noise of drones to humans, wildlife, and domestic animals. Failure to stick by the rules and be considerate impacts the wider drone photography community and may lead to tougher regulations in future.

Drones offer a huge range of creative opportunities to the imaginative photographer, so go out and have fun!

Fergus Kennedy

TIPS

- Polarizers and variable neutral density (ND) filters remove reflections, so avoid using these types of filters.

- Be aware that your drone's downward-positioning sensors may get confused when flying low over water and lead to erratic movement, although this should only be an issue when you have overhead obstructions that reduce GPS signal.

ASSIGNMENT JOURNAL

_____

_____

_____

_____

_____

_____

_____

_____

_____

▶ *The waves mean that the reflections are indistinct and impressionistic, but they still add atmosphere to this image of chalk cliffs.*

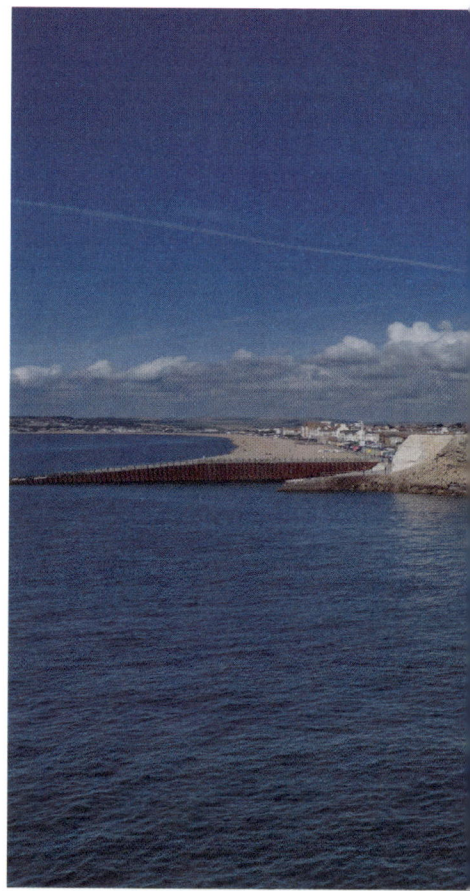

ON REFLECTION

Drones give you the ability to fly over bodies of water and achieve viewpoints that you couldn't otherwise, making capturing beautiful reflections so much easier.

Your first assignment is to use your drone to shoot a subject and its reflection. If the water is dead calm and flat, you will get a mirrorlike reflection. If there is wind and the water is rippled, you will get an increasingly impressionistic reflection. Both approaches can produce pleasing results, although if you have a mirrorlike reflection, you may want to consider a symmetrical composition. If the subject resembles an abstract splash of color in the water, however, you might want to be more creative when framing your shot.

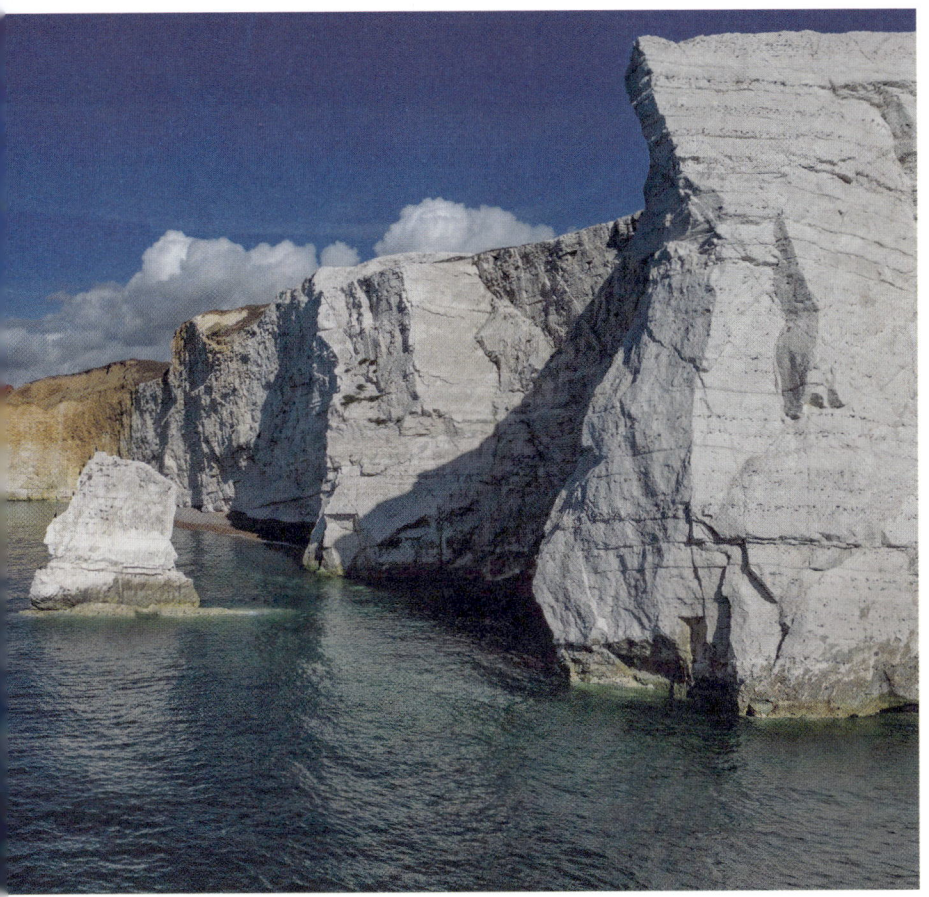

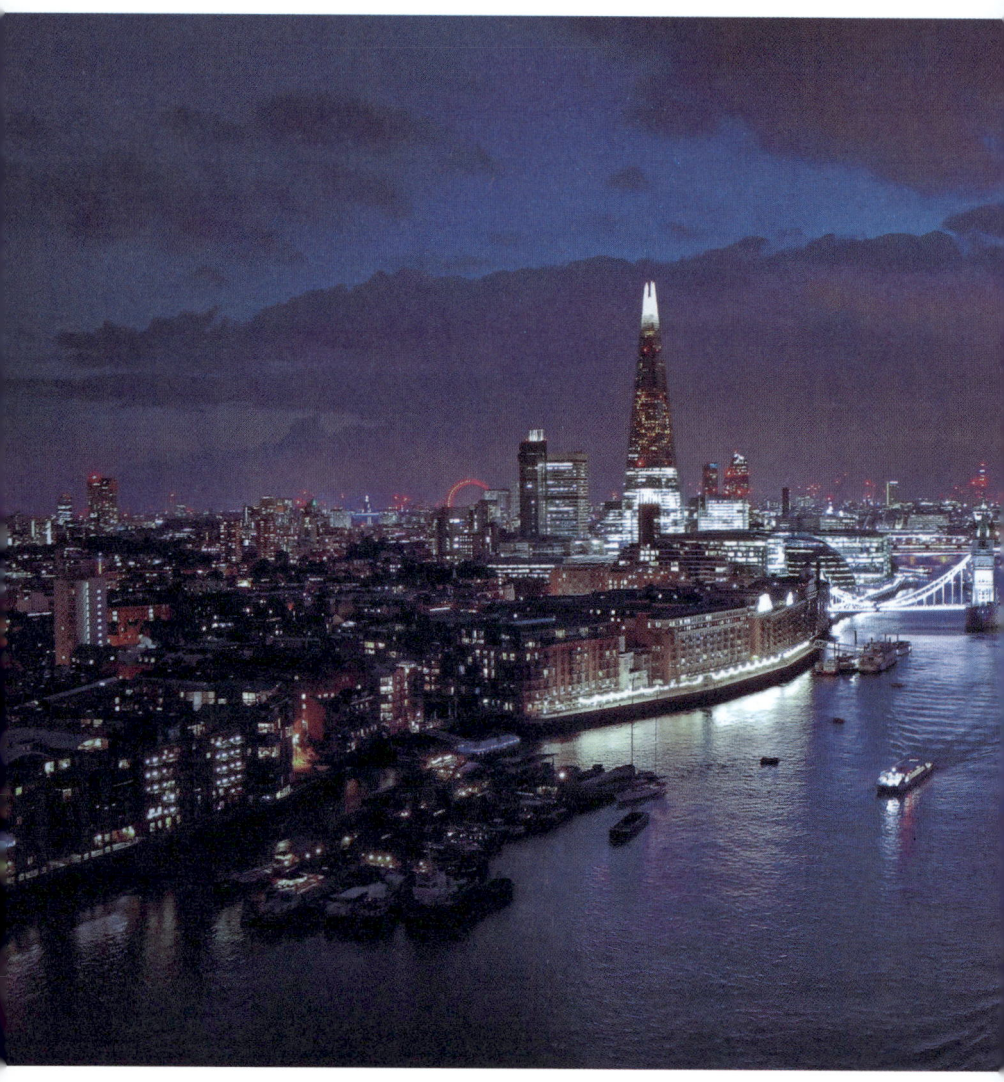

TECHNIQUE

To keep reflections sharp, avoid very slow shutter speeds. This may limit your options in low-light or night situations, but you can always operate with the aperture wide open (if your drone has this option) and an ISO as high as you find acceptable (800 or 1600 should be fine). Shutter speeds slower than 1/2 sec. will produce increasingly blurred reflections, but this can produce a pleasingly abstract aesthetic.

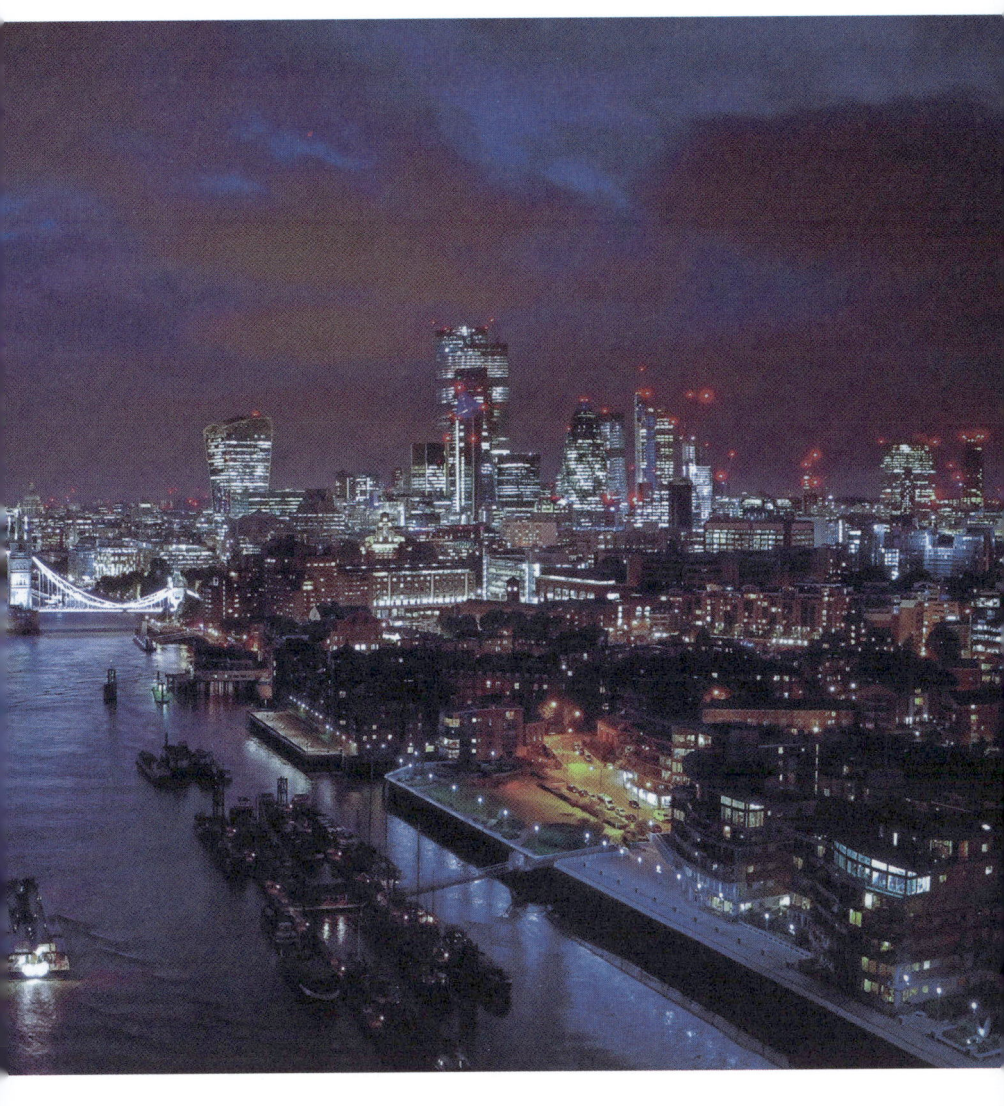

▲ *City lights make great reflections on the river and add significantly to the atmosphere.*

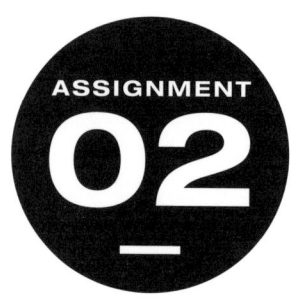

ASSIGNMENT
02

TIPS

- Consider using a neutral density (ND) filter if you are running into problems with overexposure. Sometimes, when the camera is looking directly into the sun, parts of the image can be too bright, even at the fastest shutter speed available.

- Late summer can be a good time from long, dry grasses really "popping" at golden hour.

▶ *These backlit grasses add some great texture to the foreground in this shot of a sunset in Komodo National Park, Indonesia.*

▶ *I positioned the sun behind the steam from the industrial chimneys to reduce the harshness of the highlights in this shot of a misty valley.*

BACKLIGHT DELIGHT

Your assignment is to take an image with the camera pointed toward the light source (usually the sun, although it could be the moon or artificial lights). This type of image is sometimes known as "contre-jour" and works particularly well if there is semitranslucent vegetation such as grasses or if there is haze or smoke in the air.

Shoot your image early morning or evening, when the sun is low in the sky but still above the horizon. Point your drone camera toward the sun (although it doesn't necessarily need to be in the frame). Try to compose your shot to show off the backlit elements, whether they be grass or leaves on trees or something else. You may find that small adjustments to the angle of the camera make a big difference to the effect, so don't be afraid to experiment. You can also get nice images where the sun is in shot and peeking through the leaves of a forest canopy.

It's easy to overexpose the sky when shooting into the light so use exposure compensation to darken the exposure by a stop or two. You can always recover some shadow detail at the post-processing stage.

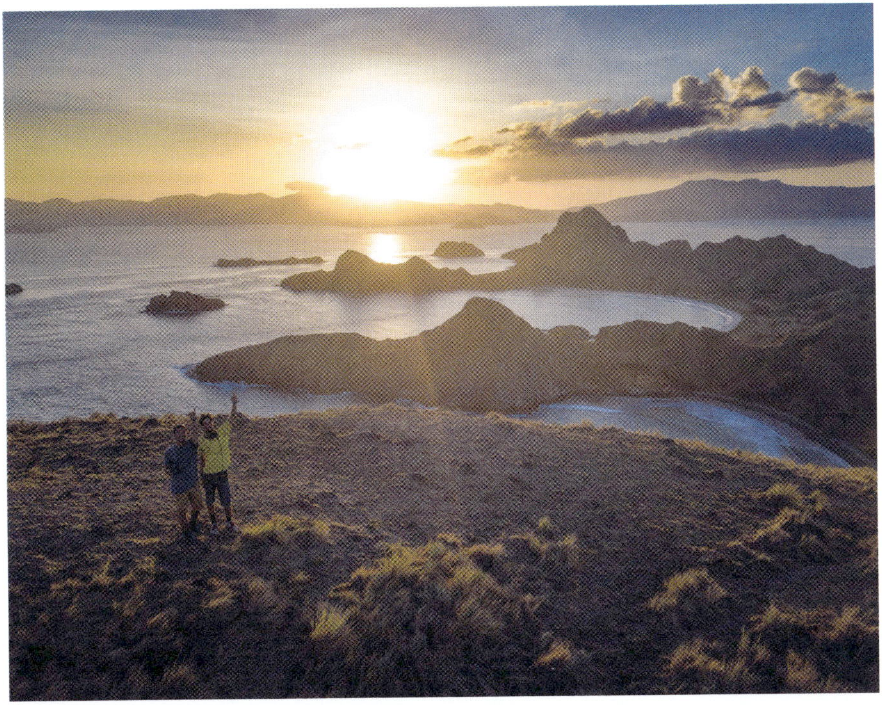

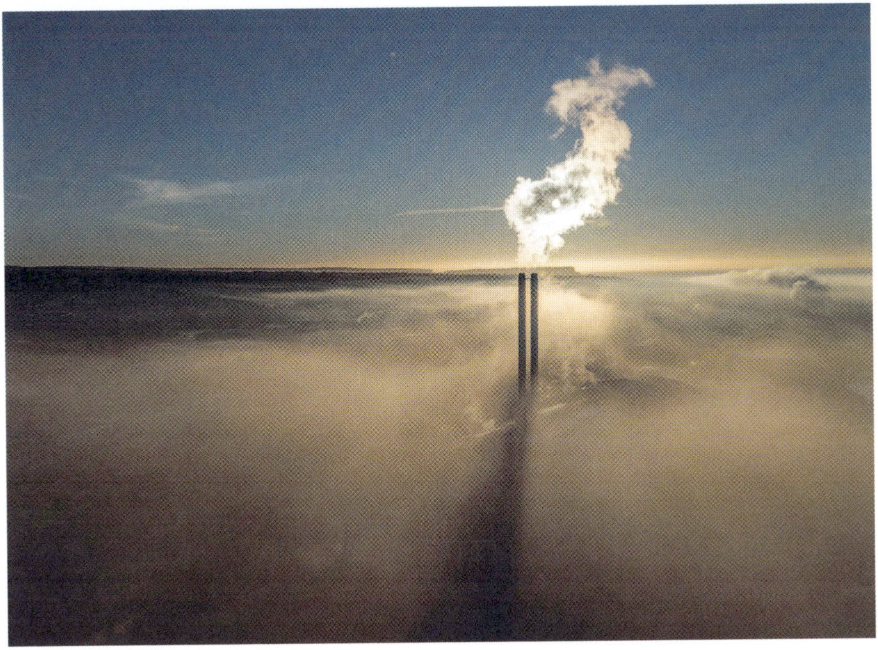

ASSIGNMENT

03

TIPS

- An abstract image is one in which the photographer focuses on a fragment of a scene, removing it from its context. Such images often concentrate on color, texture, and shape.

- If the area you want to capture is too large to fit in the field of view from your maximum height, consider taking several overlapping images and stitching them together.

▼ *I liked the curve in this loch shoreline. The combination of vegetation, pebbles, seaweed, and water gives a nice set of textures.*

▶ *A light sprinkling of snow served to accentuate the dark water in the channels.*

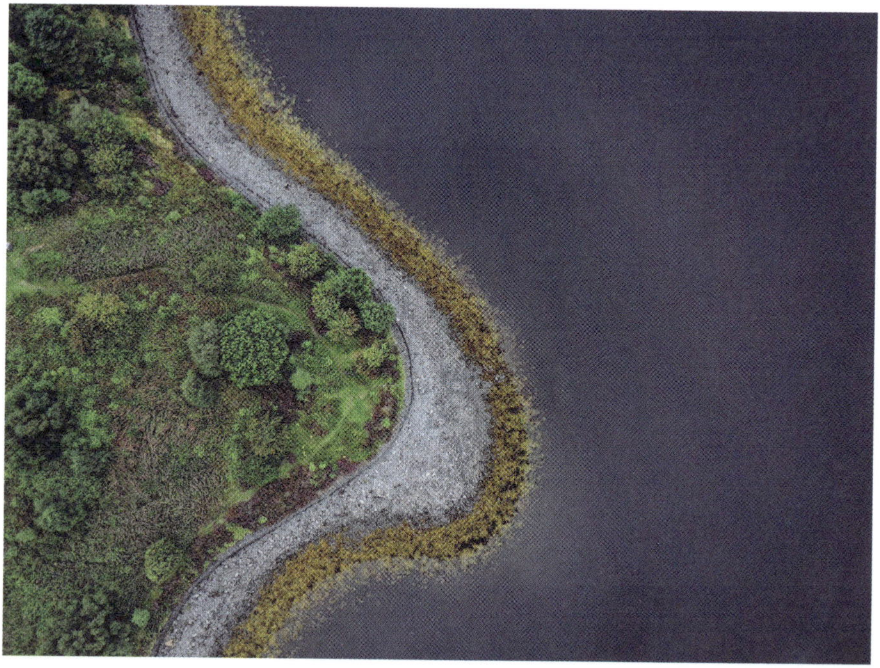

ABSTRACT NATURE

You can find a myriad of fascinating colors, textures, and patterns in nature and many of them can only be appreciated from above. For this reason, you can easily miss great opportunities that are right on your doorstep. Satellite imagery often reveals interesting opportunities and will help you to gauge the scale of the area of interest so you can get some idea of the composition that is achievable. For this assignment, you will take an intriguing abstract drone image of a natural subject that leaves viewers guessing.

You may find natural abstract patterns in any sort of environment, but beaches, coastlines, estuaries, rivers, and lakes can be productive. As ever, check for any drone flight restrictions in advance but pay particular attention to nature reserves and sites of special scientific interest, as coasts and wetlands may be breeding or feeding grounds for birds.

Once you have your drone at an altitude that includes what you want to fit in, and the camera is tilted down vertically, you can adjust the yaw and make small shifts on the positioning to fine-tune your composition. As the drone will likely be quite high and possibly exposed to wind, check your settings for a sufficient shutter speed if light levels are low. If necessary, increase the ISO to compensate.

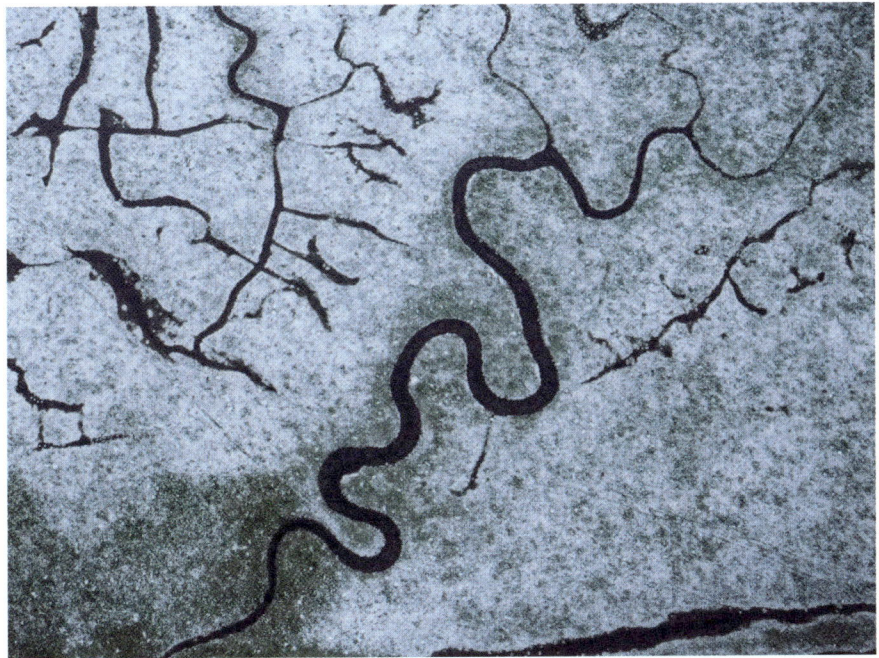

TIPS

- Use a fast shutter speed to freeze the action, preferably 1/500 sec. or faster, depending on the sport.

- Make sure you have the full consent of the players and, if possible, avoid hovering directly overhead of people for extended periods, just in case of drone malfunction.

- Take lots of images so you can select the best player positions afterward.

TOP-DOWN SPORTS

This assignment requires you to make a creative image of people playing a sport from directly above. This unfamiliar angle can produce striking images, but pay attention to your composition, taking care to line up any markings on the court, pitch, or field so that it looks deliberate. They don't have to be perpendicular or parallel—diagonals can look good too—but take time to find a pleasing composition.

If you shoot in bright sunlight, you can capture strong shadows of the players and perhaps even the ball if you're lucky. For this reason, it may take a little planning to find a suitable location, weather conditions, and players that are willing to participate. Even an empty tennis court or basketball court can make a nice abstract composition—you could even put yourself in the shot to provide a focal point.

ASSIGNMENT JOURNAL

▶ *I framed this tennis court to include the whole court and waited until the players were nicely positioned and casting interesting shadows.*

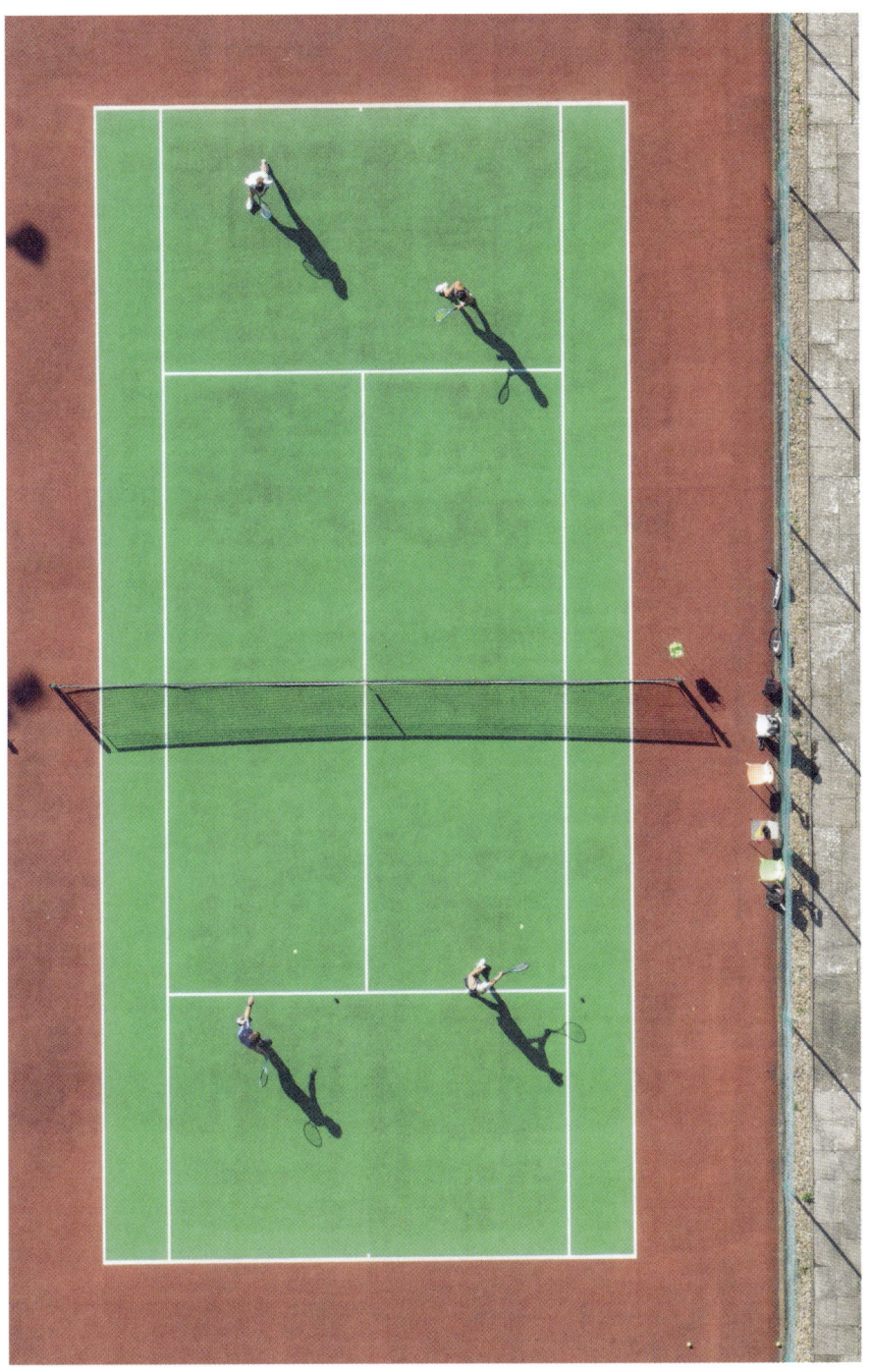

TIPS

- Be aware of the regulations where you live and make sure your flight is safe and legal. Regulations will depend on the size of your drone but always maintain a safe distance from people and try to minimize or avoid flying directly above people.

- Choose times of the day when the streets are quieter to minimize interference with traffic or pedestrians.

- Auto exposure should do a decent job but take care not to overexpose any white areas. Dialing in some negative exposure compensation should do the trick.

TOP-DOWN URBAN

Our everyday urban environment is full of fascinating shapes, colors, and textures when viewed from an unusual angle. Your assignment is to take a top-down drone photograph of an urban subject—this could include road markings, street furniture, parks, or buildings. Try to create an interesting abstract composition that shows familiar sights from a very unfamiliar perspective.

In terms of lighting conditions, flat light on an overcast day will produce a low-contrast image devoid of shadows. This may help if you want a flat, abstract look. Conversely, bright sunshine will produce strong shadows that add to the sense of depth.

Think about how any linear features line up with the edges of the frame and try small adjustments in framing by changing the altitude, yaw, and positioning of the drone. You may want to start with a high, wide shot to identify areas of interest, then either fly closer for a tighter shot or zoom in if your drone has that capability.

▶ *There's something very pleasing about the orderly grids of parking spaces when seen from above. The lower shot is a tighter detail of the scene above—the road markings add interest.*

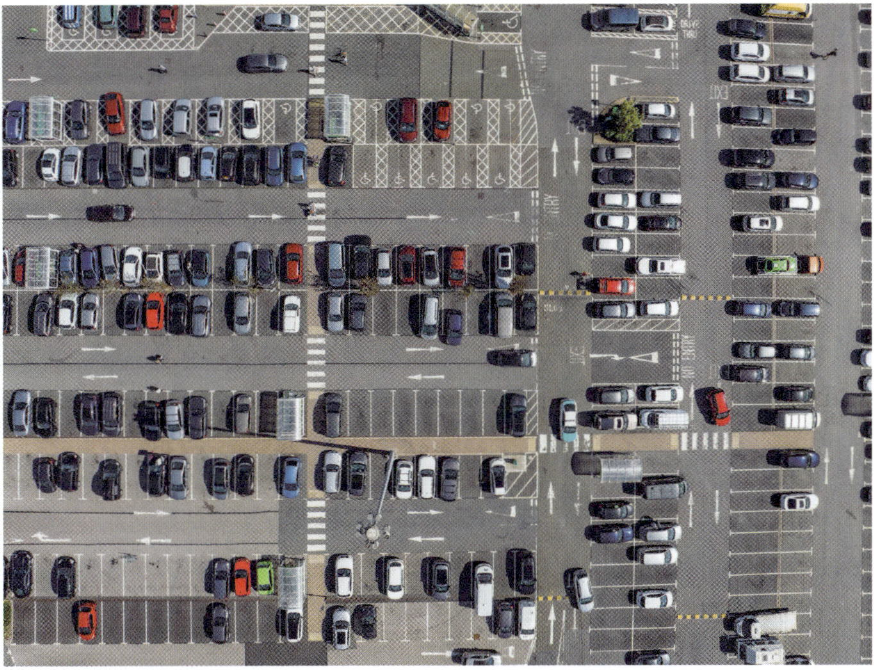

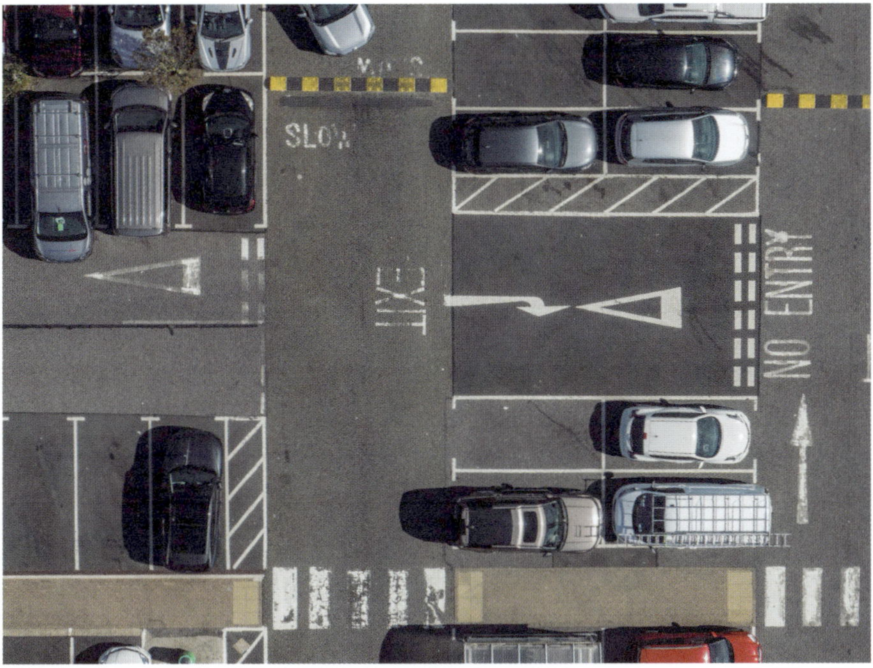
SLOW
EXIT
NO ENTRY

ASSIGNMENT
06

TIPS

- For safety, try to fly the drone so you're not underneath it. Although rare, drones have been known to occasionally lose power and fall out of the sky.
- Sunglasses help with maintaining sight of the drone if there's a bright sun overhead.

TOP-DOWN SELFIE

For this assignment, you'll break free of the arm's-length limitations of a regular selfie by snapping a drone selfie, taking advantage of your drone's unique aerial perspective to far surpass your smartphone's creative capabilities. First, find an interesting location and try to imagine a composition that would look good with a person lying in the frame, or you could remain standing and make an interesting shadow. Ideas that might work include a jetty or breakwater, a tennis or basketball court, rock formations, or other interesting natural textures.

If it's at all sunny, you'll be squinting to keep a line of sight to the drone, so bring sunglasses. Take off and get the composition roughly right before getting yourself into position. Try a few different poses. You can keep the controller in one hand, with a finger on the shutter button, so you don't have to be looking at the screen when the image is taken. It's worth trying several different compositions at different heights, so your human figure is at a variety of sizes in the frame.

Finally, make sure you're safe—don't become a statistic of those who have lost their lives for a cool selfie.

POST-PROCESSING

Processing should be straightforward, but one thing you may want to try is either a subtle vignette to draw attention to your subject or to subtly increase the exposure and clarity around yourself.

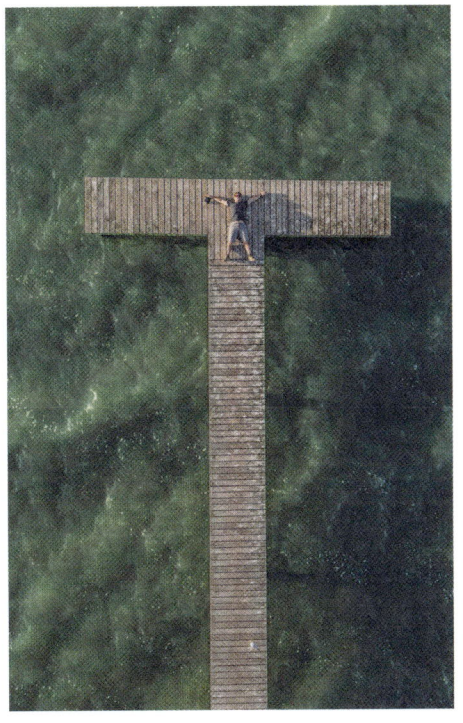

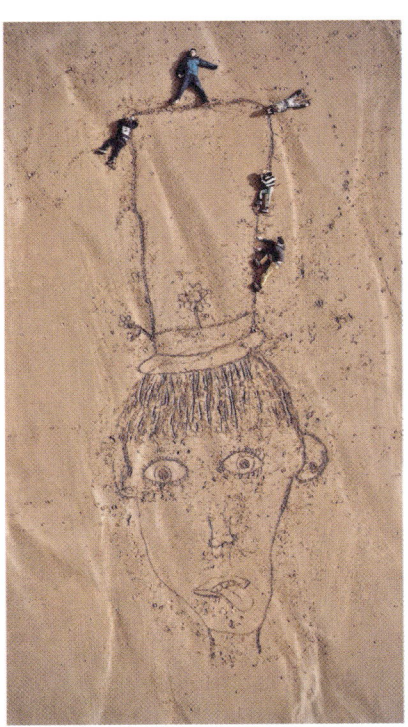

▲ Having spotted the interesting shape of the jetty, I made this selfie at a lake in New Zealand. I've increased the clarity and saturation of the water to make it look more appealing.

▲ Don't be afraid to get creative and playful—drawing images in the sand then posing with them can be very entertaining for all the family!

ASSIGNMENT JOURNAL

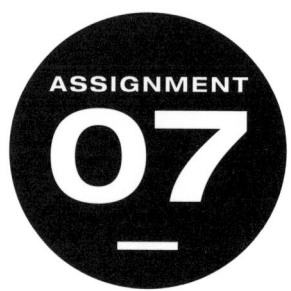

ASSIGNMENT
07

TIPS

- Check the best time of day for light on the building. Find the building using satellite imagery and check the various elevations with respect to the sun direction.

- Consider privacy and ask for permission —depending on circumstances, you may be able to make contact in advance or knock on the door on the day.

BUILDING A REPUTATION

Sometimes, the best way to appreciate architecture is from an elevated perspective and, in this assignment, your task is to find an interesting structure in your neighborhood that makes you think of it in a way you've never considered from ground level. Look for the most eye-catching features of the building, particularly those that can only be seen from the air—some buildings have a surprising footprint when viewed from above.

As with most subjects, lighting is key, so do some prior research as to what the best side of the building is aesthetically and at what time of day it is best illuminated. In the northern hemisphere, even north-facing buildings may get some illumination in midsummer, very early morning, and late evening. If not, you may be able to get a pleasing backlit shot. As ever, make sure you're flying legally, particularly in urban areas where there may be airspace restrictions—the shots featured here were taken for the architect and carried out with full permission from the appropriate government authority and the local police. Even after the legal checks are done, always be considerate and if you are flying near windows, let people know your plans.

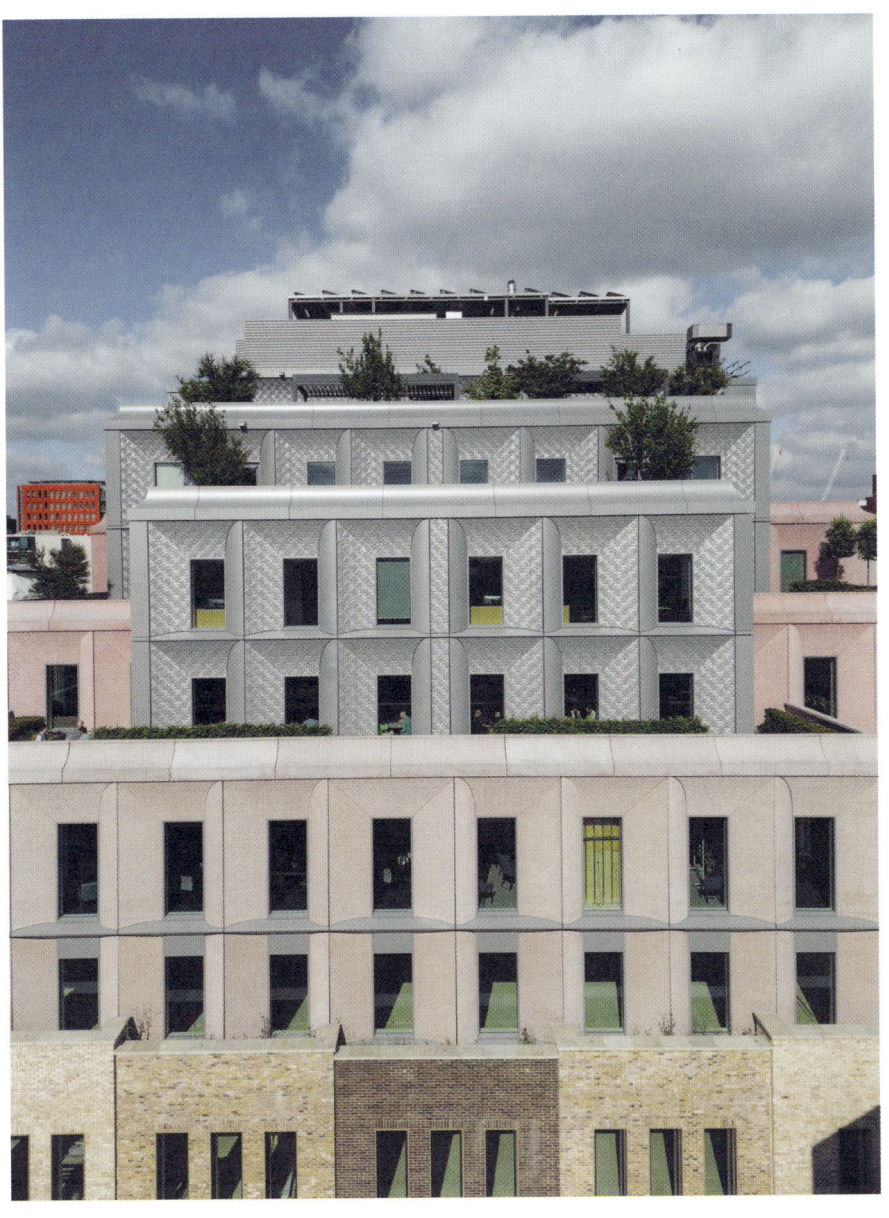

▲ *A front elevation of MATT Architecture's Ilona Rose House. For this shot, the drone had to be directly above another row of buildings. It's a perspective you can't get any other way.*

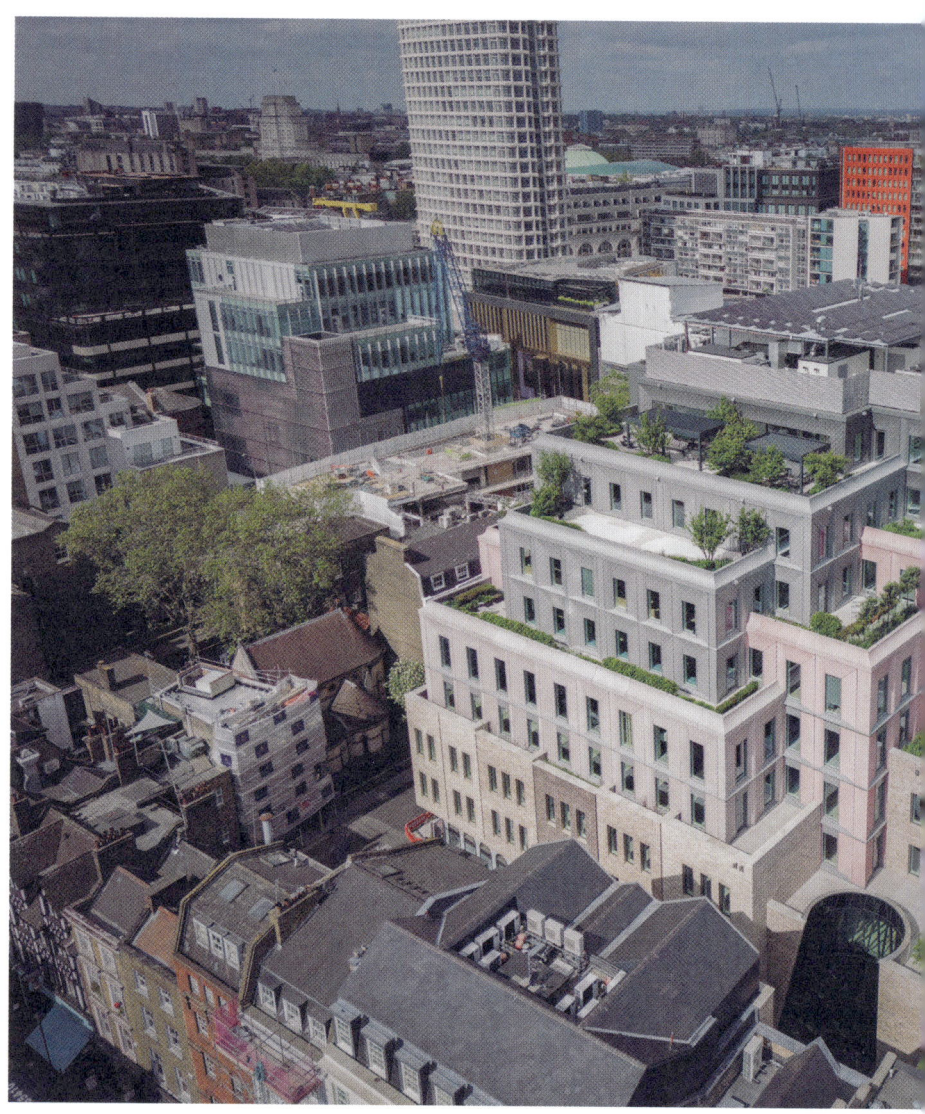

Once airborne, explore the angles. Sometimes, the best composition might not be the one you planned. Work with the shapes and geometry of the building. For instance, a square-on elevation might be the most impactful view. For this, you'll want to have the drone centered on the midpoint of the building, perpendicular to the wall. Alternatively, you might favor a diagonal view from an elevated perspective.

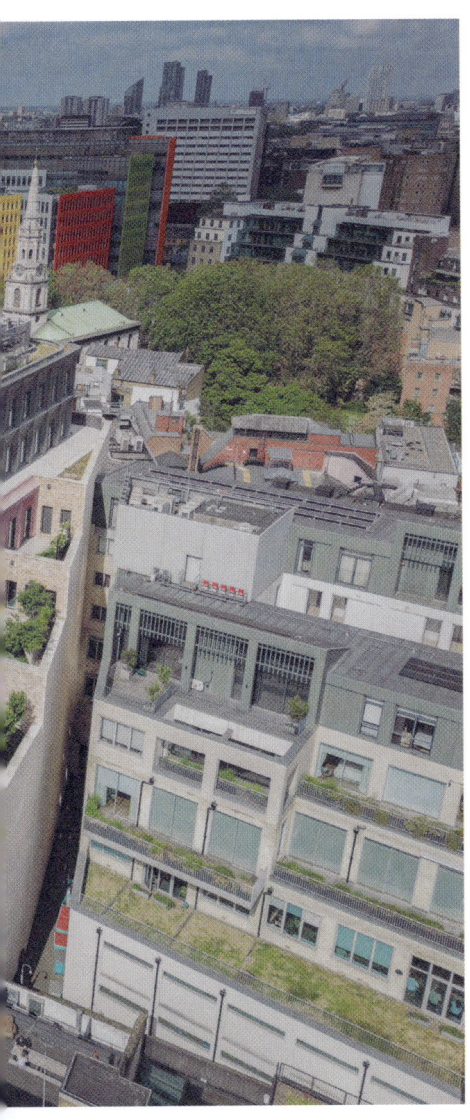

◄ An elevated diagonal perspective that showcases the terraces.

ASSIGNMENT JOURNAL

POST-PROCESSING

Aside from the usual basic corrections, you may want to use a little clarity and dehaze in architectural shots. Also, if you are bothered by converging or diverging verticals on wide lenses, you can apply some correction (using the "vertical" slider in the transform section of your processing software).

ASSIGNMENT

08

TIPS

- Try to shoot in lighter winds, as your drone will remain stiller in the air during longer exposures.

- If you use Auto ISO, you can adjust your shutter speed but keep the same overall exposure. Just check it doesn't get too high, as this will introduce unwanted noise into your images. An ISO of 800 or lower should be fine with most drones.

- Zoom in on your phone or remote display to check sharpness before taking your shot. Reviewing your images on location will save you from having to reshoot if you find imperfections at the editing stage.

BLURRING NATURE

This assignment invites you to shoot a natural subject and use motion blur to introduce a sense of movement in an otherwise still photo. You will need to have good manual control of your settings, especially shutter speed. Waterfalls or waves make good subjects for motion blur, and it makes sense to include static subjects in the composition so that it's not the whole image that appears soft and blurry.

Experiment with shutter speeds until you find the optimum balance between static objects and a sense of motion in the moving elements. Balancing your exposure may require you to shoot in low light or use a strong neutral density (ND) filter.

TECHNIQUE

If you don't have a filter, shoot either after sunset or before sunrise and aim for shutter speeds between 1/10 sec. and 2 sec., checking your results and adjusting accordingly. Very long exposures give a smooth, misty look to moving water, while shorter exposures will show more detail in the movement, for instance individual flying droplets with a trail behind them.

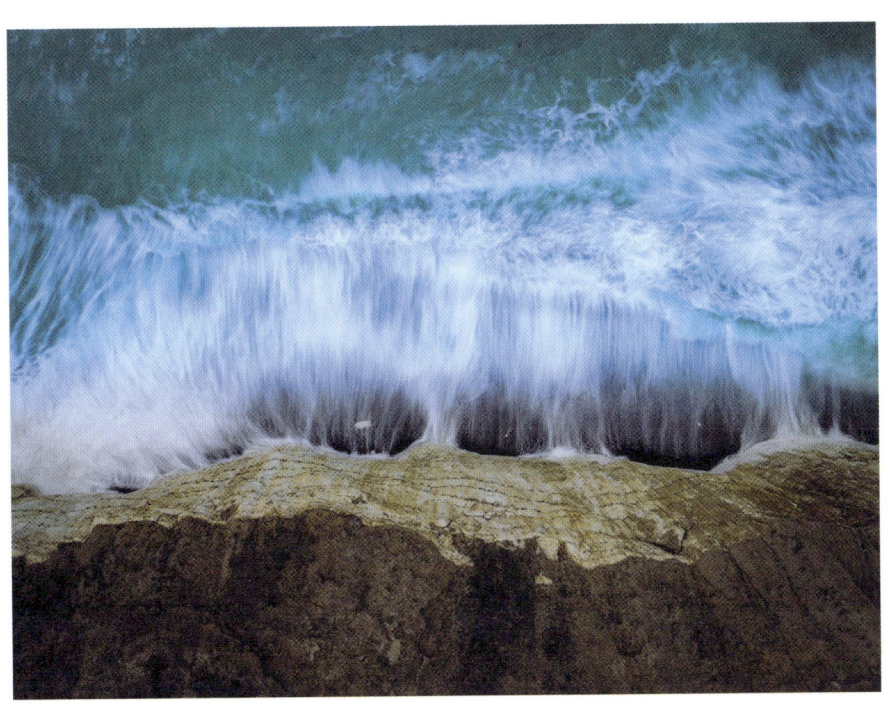

▲ *I used a shutter speed of 1/10 sec. to achieve some good motion blur in this shot of waves crashing on a beach under the cliffs.*

ASSIGNMENT JOURNAL

TIPS

- You may need to use Sport Mode to get sufficient speed but be aware that obstacle avoidance is disabled in this mode.

- Flying closer to the ground will increase the motion blur effect, but be careful—things happen quickly when you're flying fast and you'll want to avoid high-speed collisions with the ground or obstacles.

- If you struggle to achieve enough motion blur safely, you may be able to enhance the effect using a motion blur filter in your editing software.

NEED FOR SPEED

Drones make ideal tools for capturing a sense of speed, as they're essentially fast-moving cameras, often capable of keeping up with moving cars and bikes. For this assignment, you'll be using a slow shutter speed to add some motion blur to the surroundings of a moving vehicle, while maintaining the vehicle itself in sharp focus.

You will need to plan your shot carefully. Decide what angle you want to shoot from—side-on can work well, as can looking back toward your subject at an angle. The best shutter speed to use will depend on the speed of your subject and your proximity to the ground. You will need to try to match the speed of the vehicle, so that it stays in the same position in the frame. For this reason, it makes sense to know the maximum speed of your drone and try to shoot a subject that's not traveling much faster than this speed. If possible, make multiple attempts using different shutter speeds until you find the optimum for your shot. I would suggest trying shutter speeds between 1/30 sec. and 1 sec.

From a safety point of view, never fly close to trains or public roads and be aware of obstacles such as trees, lampposts, and telegraph poles, particularly when flying sideways. As ever, comply with the local drone regulations wherever you are flying.

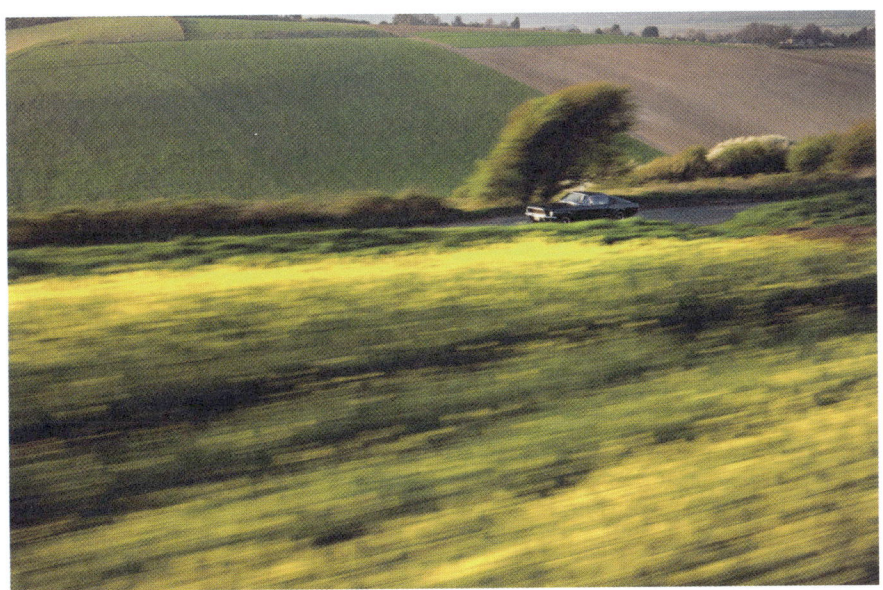

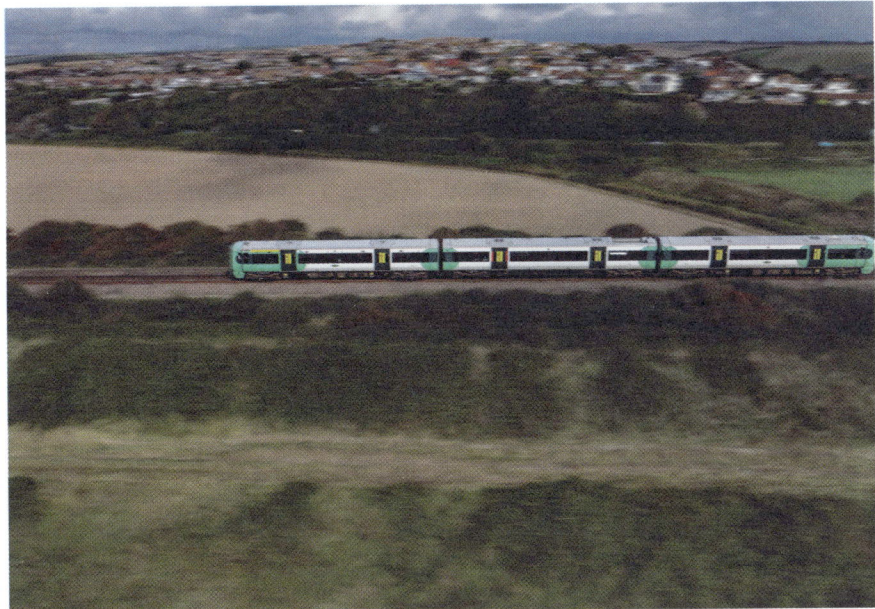

▲ ▲ I used a 1/10 sec. shutter speed for this shot of a Mustang speeding alongside fields of flowers.

▲ This train was shot at 1/30 sec. at full speed on the drone. Because of the altitude, the motion blur effect was limited, so I've added a little extra in Photoshop.

ASSIGNMENT
10

TIPS

- Like your smartphone, your drone may have zoom settings (either digital or optical) on the interface, typically near the record/shutter button, such as 1x, 3x, and 7x.

- Learn to spot interesting areas of detail in the wider view—the widest setting provides a great scouting tool.

ZOOM IN

The wideangle perspective of the lens on many drones can lend a similar look to most drone images. However, you do have options. Some drones have a zoom function, which may be optical or digital or a combination of both. This feature allows you to zero in on an area of interest without having to get too close. The more "telephoto" perspective will also change the look of an image, giving a foreshortening effect, where background elements are relatively larger. Even without the in-camera options, you can, of course, move the drone closer and/or crop in post-processing. Note that any digital zoom or crop will reduce the effective resolution of your image.

Compositionally, you will be looking for different features compared to the usual wideangle image. For your assignment, look for a main subject to concentrate on—possible subject matter might include a prominent or unusual building, a landscape feature, tree, or maybe a vehicle of some sort.

The more "telephoto" your shot is, the more careful you will have to be with shutter speed, as motion blur becomes more of an issue. This will particularly be the case for low-light shots. The optimum exposure length will depend on how windy it is and how much zoom you are using, but as a rule of thumb, in low light shutter speed may be anything from 1/50 sec. to 1 sec. Any longer and you will struggle to get sharp shots.

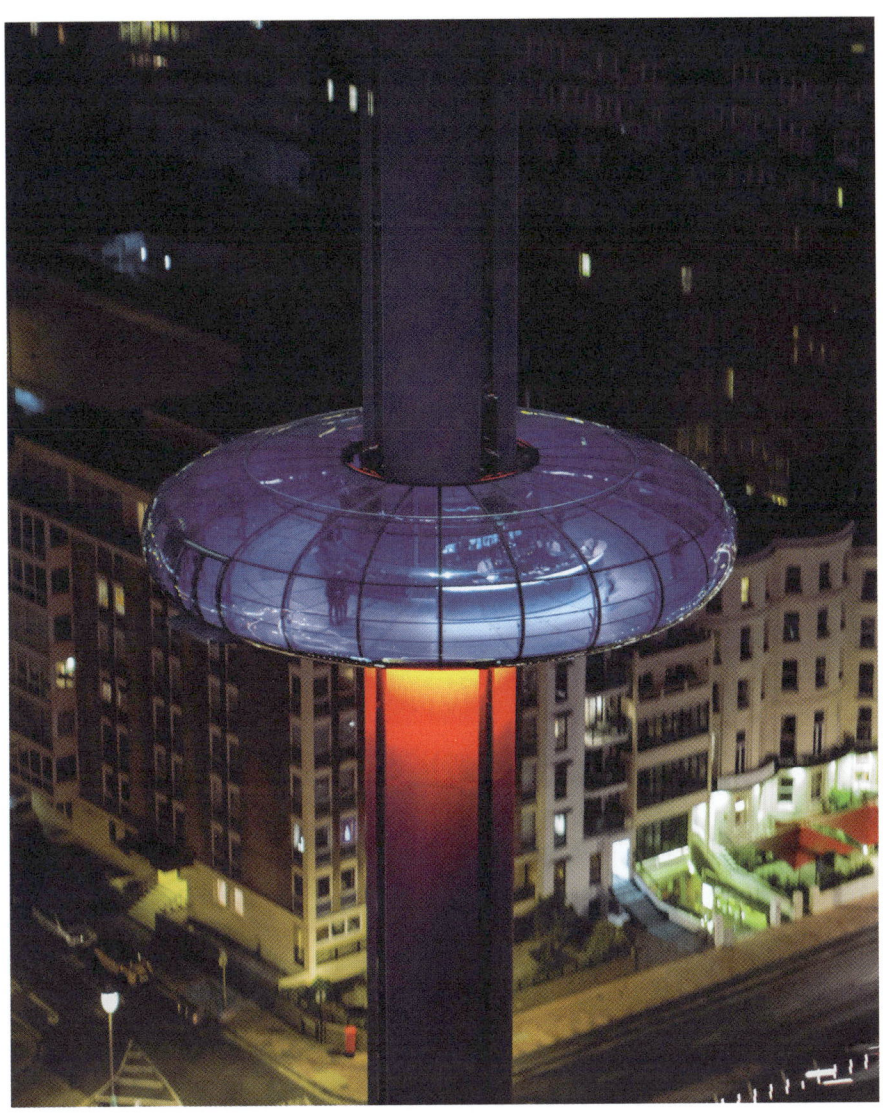

▲ *This observation tower's capsule was moving, so I used a slow shutter speed and tried to match the speed of ascent with my drone, hence the slight motion blur of the background. This was shot with the 35mm equivalent of a 90mm lens.*

ASSIGNMENT
11

TIPS

- Use a free global weather app such as the Weather Channel or AccuWeather to plan your shoot—overcast days that produce softer shadows are best.

- Ensure you have sufficient space on all sides of your subject to orbit it at various heights, while fitting the full structure in the frame.

MAKE A 3D MODEL

Using a technique called photogrammetry, it's possible to make a 3D model of an object. The output is an interactive digital model that can be orientated on any axis by the viewer. A drone makes an ideal tool for this task, as not only can it move in 3D space to shoot an object from all angles, but the images are also geotagged with their exact location in the metadata. Your assignment is to produce a 3D model of a building or structure using your drone.

A building makes a great subject for a 3D model, but a statue or monument or even a tree could work. The input for the model is a series of still images from many angles. You should capture one "nadir" image—that is a photo centered on the building, looking directly down, where the building fills the frame nicely. Next, you need to fly three orbits of the building at differing altitudes, capturing full-resolution still images as you go. The lowest orbit should have the camera as close to horizontal as possible whilst flying safely with the building centred in frame. Aim to have the camera around 45° for the second orbit and 75° downward for the third.

These numbers are just for guidance, and you don't need to stick to them exactly. On each orbit, the more images the better—you might capture 30 to 100 or more per orbit depending on the size of your subject. You can take fewer and still get a working model, but the more you have, the more precise your results will be.

▶ *This house is ideal for making into a 3D model, as it has plenty of space around it, although one side is partly obscured by trees.*

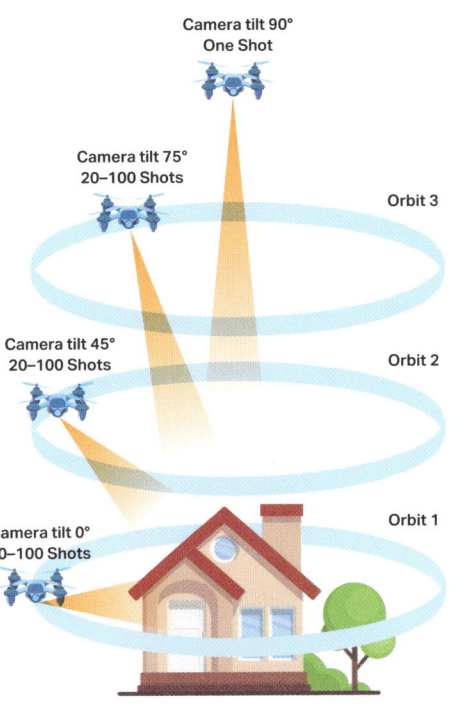

Camera tilt 90°
One Shot

Camera tilt 75°
20–100 Shots

Orbit 3

Camera tilt 45°
20–100 Shots

Orbit 2

Camera tilt 0°
20–100 Shots

Orbit 1

POST-PROCESSING

Input images are fed into software that constructs a 3D "point cloud"—a distribution of surface points in 3D space—then drapes imagery over the point cloud. Various software is available, such as Pix4D and DroneDeploy, both of which operate on the cloud and offer free trials. Also look at Colmap, MicMac, Meshroom, and Agisoft Metashape, which are all free.

Once you've completed and exported your 3D model, you can share it online at sketchfab.com, a 3D-modeling platform.

◄ *Suggested flight paths for 3D-modeling imagery. Aim for 20 to 100 images per orbit.*

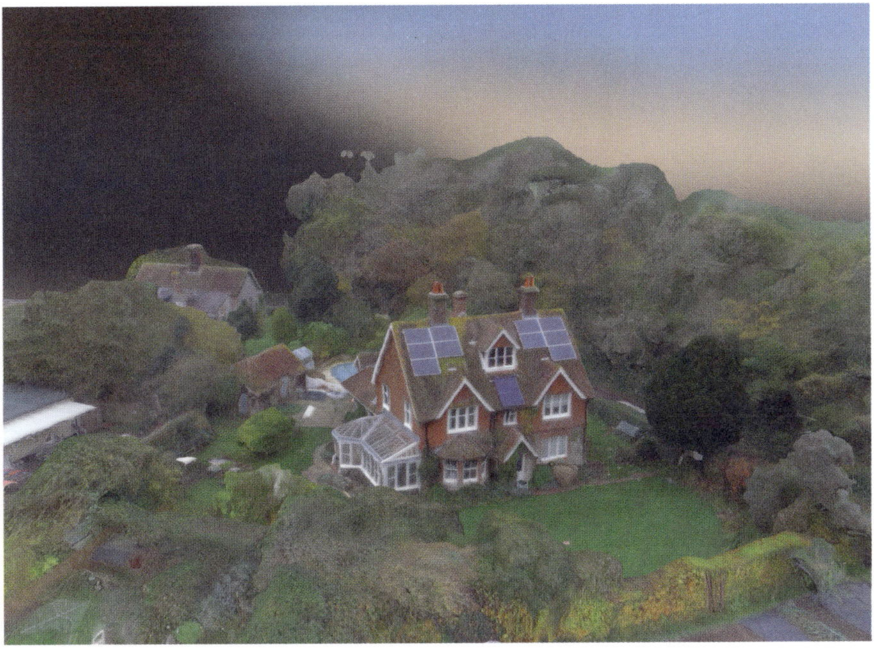

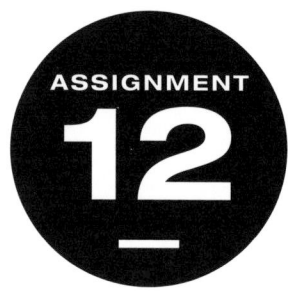

ASSIGNMENT

12

TIPS

• Before you get started, it helps to familiarize yourself with ground-based long-exposure photography using a tripod. Go to your selected subject at night and experiment with long exposure times until you get a good exposure setting.

• Some drones feature an inbuilt downward-facing LED light that you can switch on in the app. If your drone doesn't have a built-in light, you can fit a small third-party LED light (make sure this doesn't interfere with the sensors or the propellers).

SPECIAL KIT

• DSLR or mirrorless camera and lens (a camera phone that allows manual long exposures would also work)

• Tripod

• Drone with LED light

ASSIGNMENT JOURNAL

_____

_____

_____

_____

_____

_____

_____

_____

▶ *I used a 60-sec. exposure to photograph this abandoned pier, with the halo created with a Lume Cube light fitted to a DJI Mavic 2 Pro.*

PUT A HALO ON IT

An unusual use for your drone is to "paint" a glowing halo-like effect above a subject which you then photograph with a ground-based camera. Your assignment is to create a long-exposure "drone halo" shot featuring a subject such as an abandoned building, a solitary tree, or an interesting rock formation.

Recce your location during the day and practice setting the drone on an automated orbit of your subject using its Point of Interest (POI) mode. Depending on your drone model, you may have the option to either select the subject on your screen or mark the subject's center point while flying directly over it. Set the duration of the 360° orbit to match your exposure time on the ground-based camera—somewhere between 30 and 60 seconds will work well. Once you have perfected the technique during daylight, you can go for the shot.

Have the ground-based camera set up and ready to go, then take off with the drone, get it in the starting position and start the long exposure. At the same time, start the drone orbit. Check the results on your camera and, if necessary, tweak the exposure and/or drone orbit.

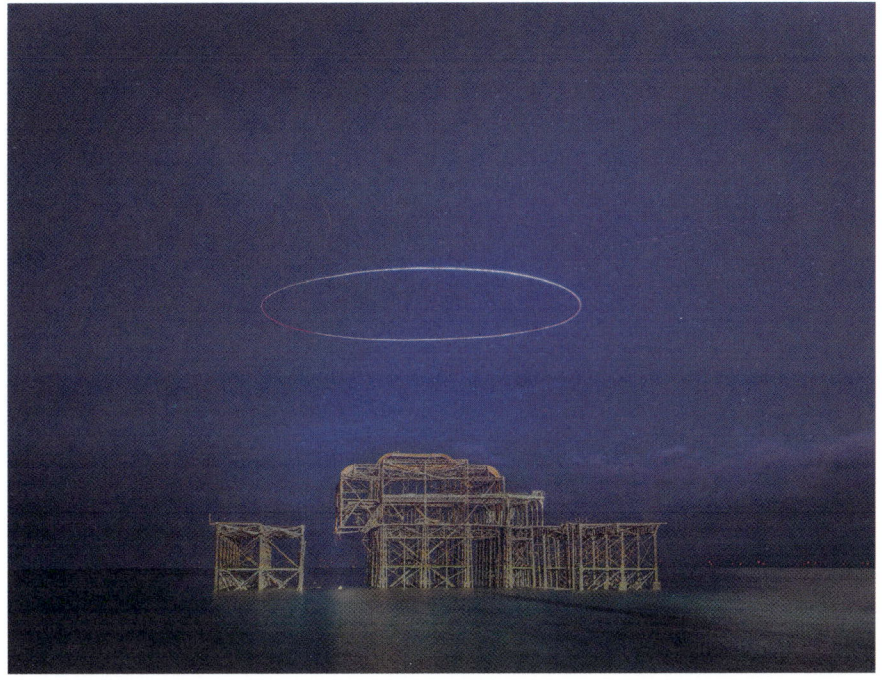

ASSIGNMENT

13

TIPS

- As much as possible, use manual settings on your ground-based camera and practice shooting from the ground at night before embarking on the full challenge of drone lighting. You will need to have full control of shutter speed, aperture, and ISO to get the best results.

- For a more advanced challenge, you could capture a long exposure (typically 10 to 30 sec.) of the stars or Milky Way and blend it with your lit foreground.

- To avoid task overload, it might be helpful to take a friend along for this assignment.

DRONE LIGHTING

For this assignment, you'll use your drone to light a subject from above while taking the photograph with a ground-level camera. Many drones have a small, downward-facing LED light that you can switch on manually in the app. Even if your drone doesn't have this feature, it may be possible to fix a small LED light to your drone—either a purpose-built light (the safer option) or a small LED flashlight fixed to the drone. If you choose the latter option, be careful to ensure the fixing doesn't interfere with the props or the sensors.

Once you've chosen your subject, recce the area in daylight, looking out for hidden obstacles and composing your shot. After dark, set up your ground-based camera on a tripod (a phone camera with night mode will work), compose your shot, and select settings for a long exposure (you might want to start with 20 sec., f/2.8, and ISO 3200). Turn on your drone light, take off, and fly into position. Then start the exposure on your ground-based camera. You can either choose to leave the drone stationary during the exposure to give hard light from a single angle or move the drone around, so your subject is lit from multiple angles.

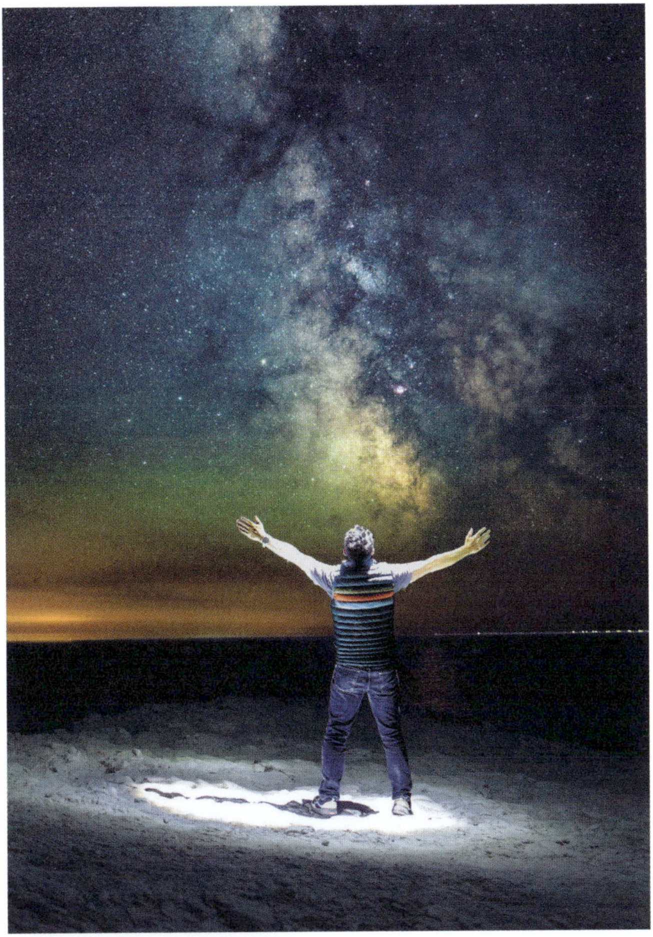

▲ The above shot blended with a tracked 2-minute exposure of the Milky Way taken from the same location on the same night.

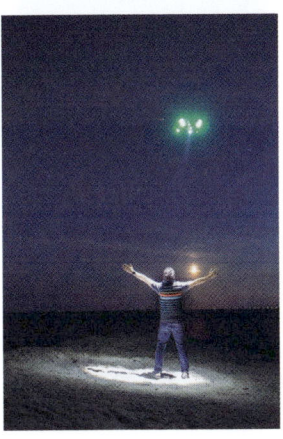

◄ I used the drone to create a sci-fi look, as if the light was coming from a UFO. I had to stay very still for a 10-sec. exposure.

ASSIGNMENT
14

TIPS

- Your hands will likely get very cold during a 15-to-20-minute flight, so gloves help, but look for some with flip-off thumb covers or just cut the thumb tips off to maintain sensitivity for the controller sticks.

- Weather apps such as Dark Sky are useful for getting an idea of the weather that's headed your way. It uses real-time radar data so you can tell if it's about to stop snowing and you can get your drone up.

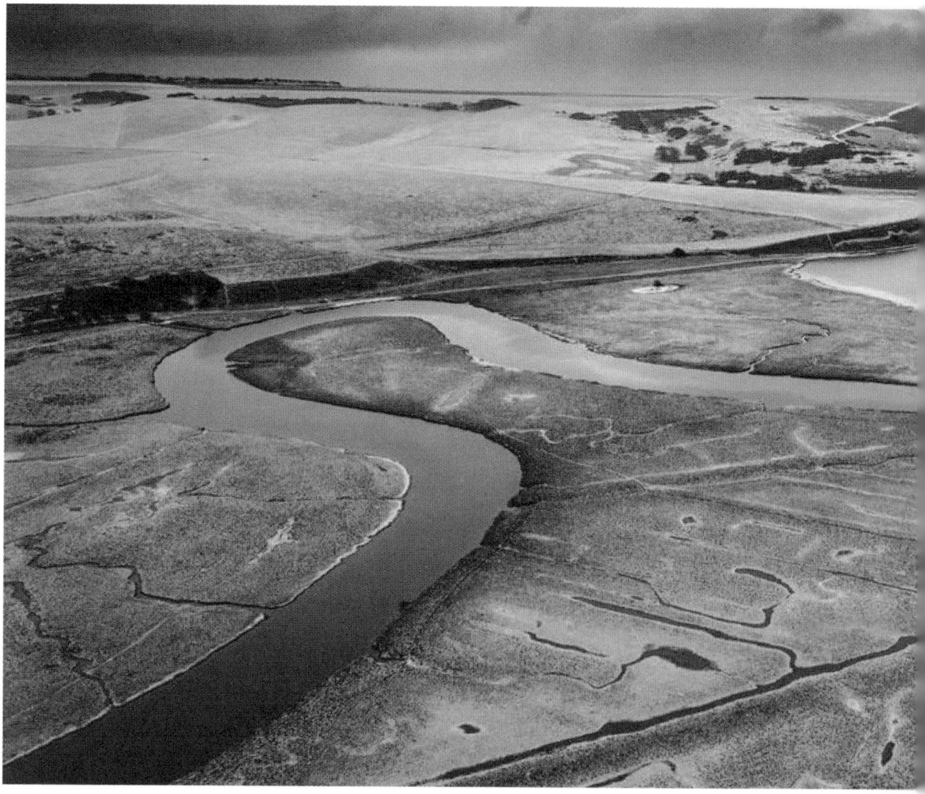

SNOW DAY

This assignment is different because depending on where you live and the time of year, you may not see the results for weeks or months. If you live in a location with regular seasonal snow cover, photographing a snowy landscape from the air should be straightforward. However, if snow cover is sometimes short-lived, it's worth visiting the location in advance and framing up the shot, taking note of height and orientation for the optimal composition. So, your task is to choose a suitable location that you think will work, and then assess your photo once the snow has fallen. Did it work as expected? Are there other locations nearby that might be more effective?

Look for features and shapes that will stand out against a white background— leafless trees and winding roads are good examples. Your composition could be quite minimal, with just a ribbon of road or river splitting the blanket of white. Keep the flight batteries and your phone warm right up to takeoff and keep an eye on exposure—if the snow is looking very bright, you might want to use negative exposure compensation to avoid blowing out the brightest areas.

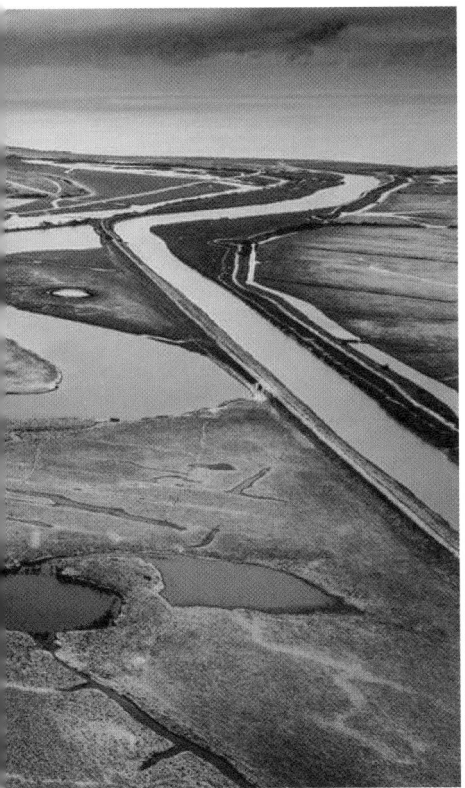

POST-PROCESSING

Snow shots often look more atmospheric with a cooler white balance setting. However, if the sun is low, a warmer white balance can also enhance the mood. For this reason, shoot in Raw for greater flexibility.

◄ *This dusting of snow only lasted a couple of hours, so it paid to be prepared and have the shot planned in advance.*

TIPS

- Keep your flight battery and phone warm in an inside pocket or inside your heated car prior to takeoff and be aware that cold conditions may reduce flight time.

- Use a landing pad to take off from to keep your lens clean, or you risk dust or moisture being blown onto the lens. Landing pads are widely available online, but a large case or camera bag might suffice.

- Select a colder white balance to enhance the frosty atmosphere.

▶ *With a dusting of frost, the grasses and branches provide some great textures in this rural landscape.*

▶ *Frost remains on the valley floor under a veil of mist long after the frost has melted on the hills.*

FROSTY LANDSCAPES

For this assignment, you will be showcasing the beauty of frosty winter weather from an aerial perspective. Familiar landscapes take on a whole new look with a dusting of frost, so keep an eye on the weather forecast and be prepared for an early start. Luckily, frosty weather often coincides with very light winds, which is always good for drone flying. The first rays of sun will often quickly melt the frost so having everything ready and settings roughly preconfigured will save vital minutes.

Once the drone is aloft, look for interesting landscape compositions and features that are accentuated by the conditions. Frosty grasses at a low angle or tree branches can look great. Valleys or depressions in the landscape will often become a frost bowl when there is a temperature inversion, so they may retain frosty conditions for longer than high areas. Also look out for patches of mist or fog.

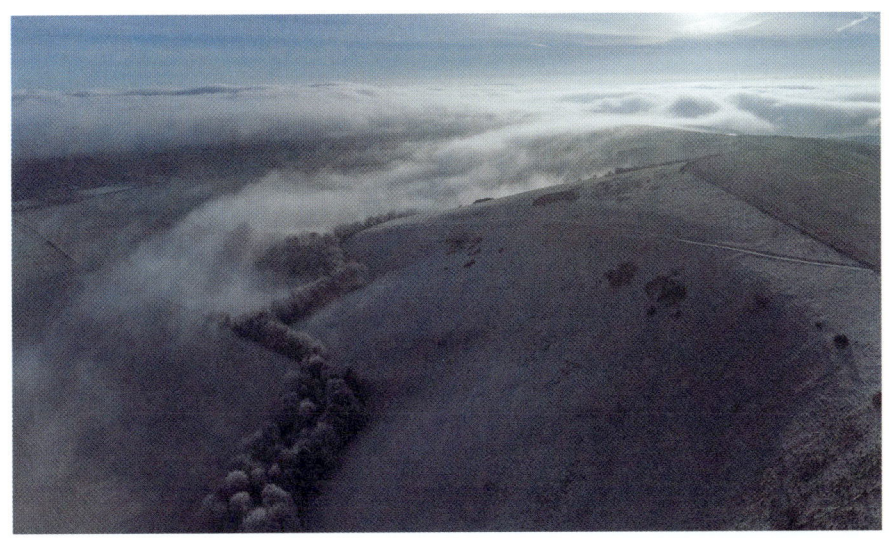

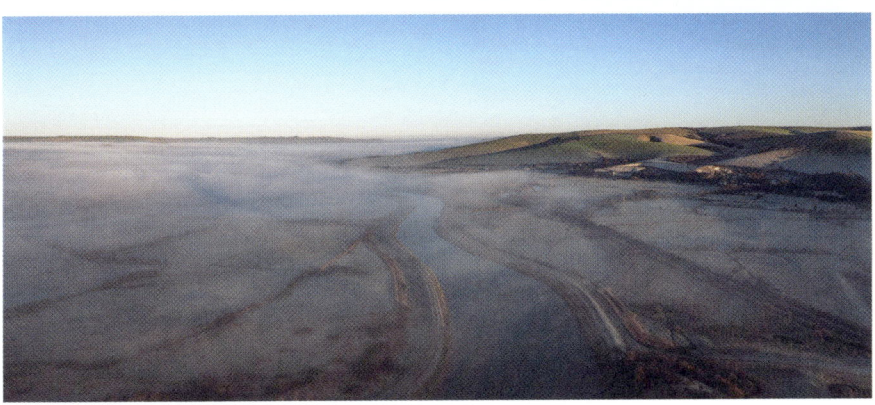

ASSIGNMENT JOURNAL

ASSIGNMENT

16

TIPS

- Find a takeoff position where you can maintain a line of sight to your drone. This is a legal requirement to help prevent collisions with other aircraft or birds.

- Consider trying a hyperlapse to capture the movement of the fog—see Assignment 27.

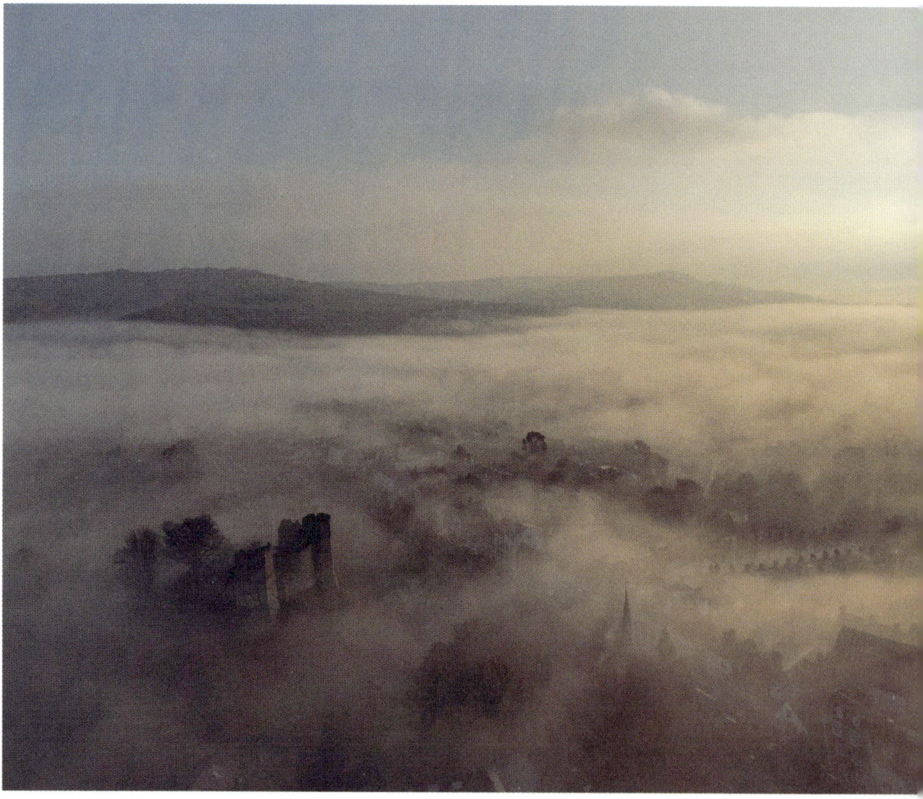

FLEETING FOG

Fog can add atmosphere and intrigue to both urban and rural settings, so for this assignment, you're going to capture a drone photograph of a landscape transformed by this mercurial weather phenomenon. Depending on your location, climatic conditions could mean that foggy spells are quite rare and fleeting. They often occur very early in the morning, so a key tip for this assignment is to be ready for a suitable weather forecast—you may get an explicit forecast for fog, but also look out for very light winds of 5 mph or less, as this makes fog more likely to form in the predawn hours. Be prepared for wasted journeys—fog is quite hard to accurately predict, so you may find you make a journey only to find no fog, or that the fog is so thick that there's no way to safely fly above it.

Fog can be very localized—low-lying areas such as river valleys can be a good bet—so identify a spot that is prone to fog, preferably one that has identifiable features such as buildings, hills, or mountains that might protrude through the fog. It can appear and vanish very quickly so it pays to have your shot and your flight planned in advance, so when the elements come together, you can get the drone in the air and in position quickly. Fog looks good predawn and/or with low light, although you'll need to pay attention to your exposure—it's easy to overexpose and blow-out parts of the fog. Patience and preparation are the key words for foggy drone photography.

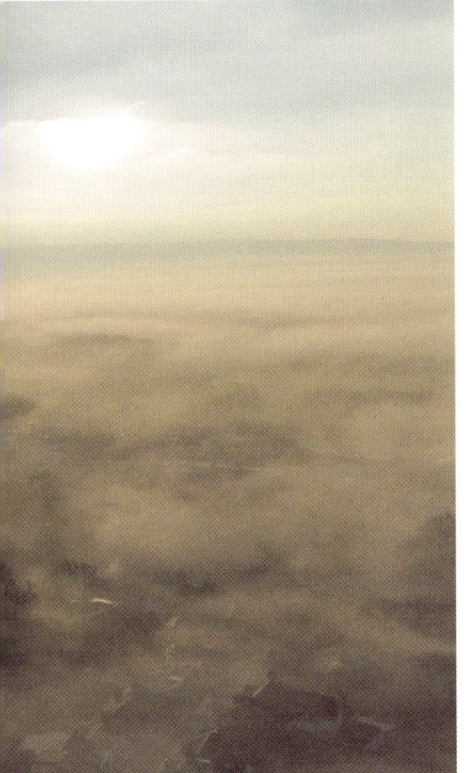

◀ *The castle protruding through the early morning fog and hints of other buildings add to the atmosphere of this scene. Timing was key in capturing just enough fog. This image is a stitched panorama of three frames.*

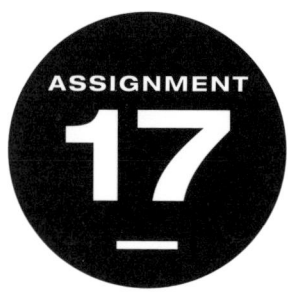

TIPS

- Carefully select the start and end frames before you start shooting. This will ensure you end up with a pleasing composition, with some downward vertical perspective at the bottom of the frame and maybe some horizon and sky at the top.

- Use Manual exposure mode and ensure the sky is not overexposed. If you use Auto, you could end up with varying exposures throughout the frame. Set your exposure so the sky is toward the right side of the histogram, but not clipping the right edge.

VERTORAMA

A vertorama is a stitched panorama on a vertical rather than horizontal axis. It's a technique that is not often seen with ground-based photography but that is particularly well-suited to drone photography. Typically, it combines a top-down image as the starting point with a more or less horizontal end point, with some sky in the frame. Your assignment is to create a successful vertorama image with some interesting features both in the top-down part and the horizon and sky.

It's a good idea to do some practice runs, framing up both the start and end of the shot. When you're ready and have checked exposure, take your vertical top-down shot, then tilt the gimbal up until you have 30–50-percent overlap with the previous frame and take another shot. Repeat this process until you reach your end frame, taking care not to touch any of the flight controls during the process. If in doubt, go beyond your end frame because you can always crop a little in post-processing.

ASSIGNMENT JOURNAL

▶ *This Scottish loch vertorama was stitched together from five source images, after adjustments to color and reducing the exposure of the sky.*

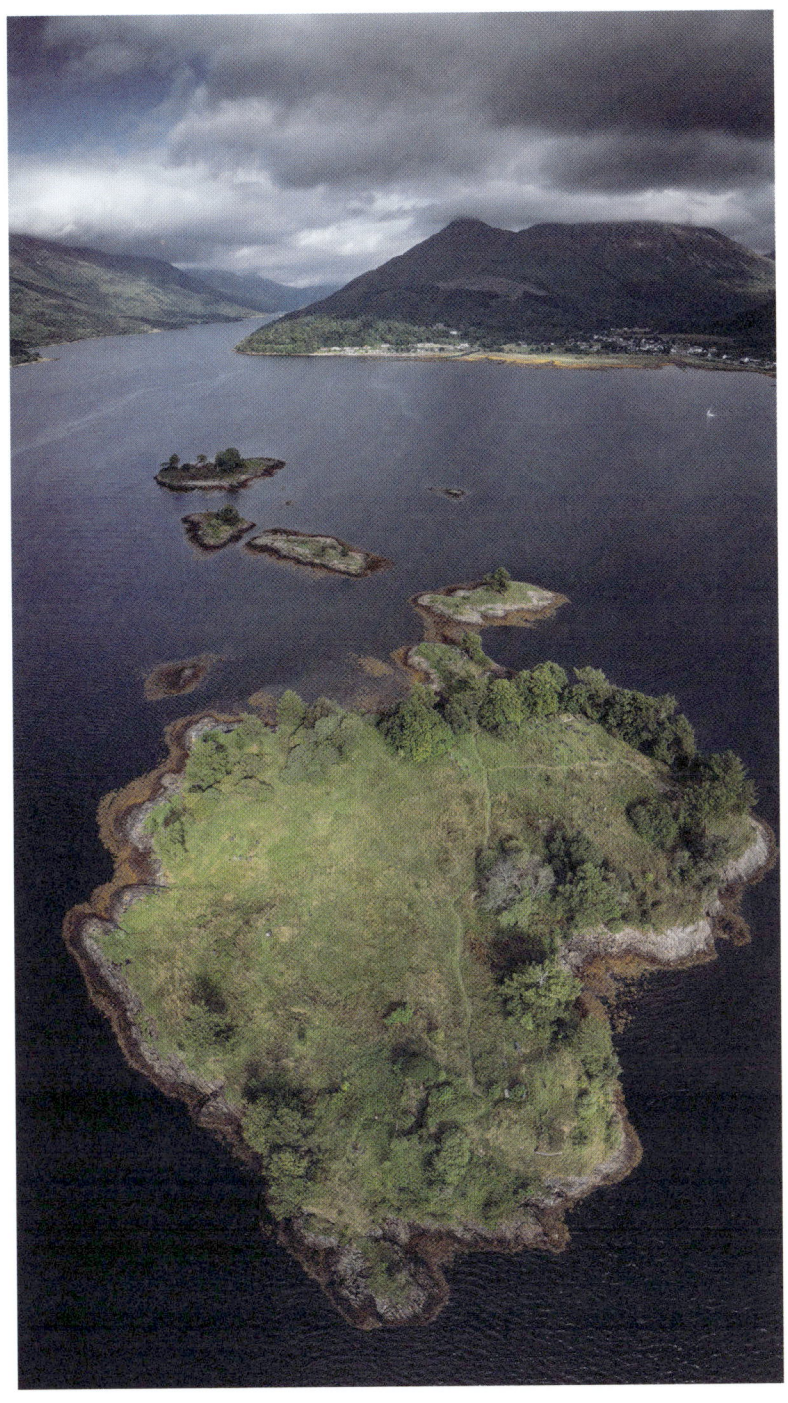

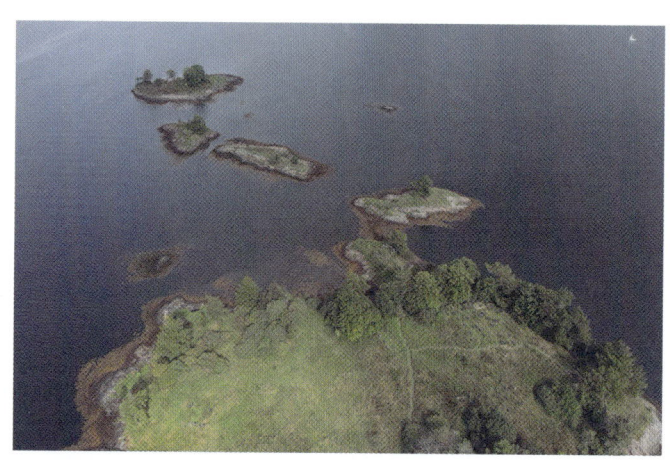

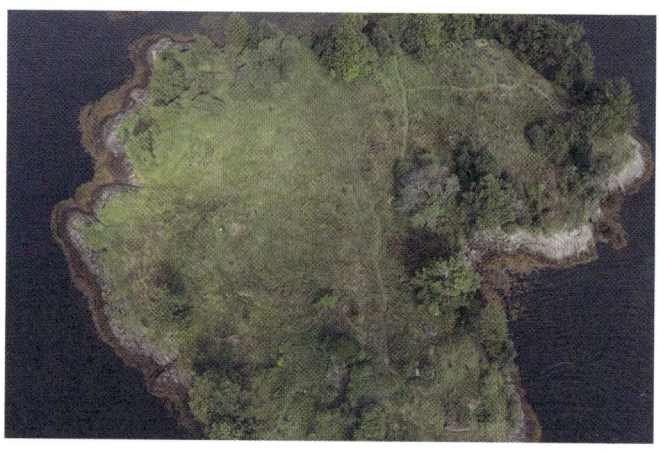

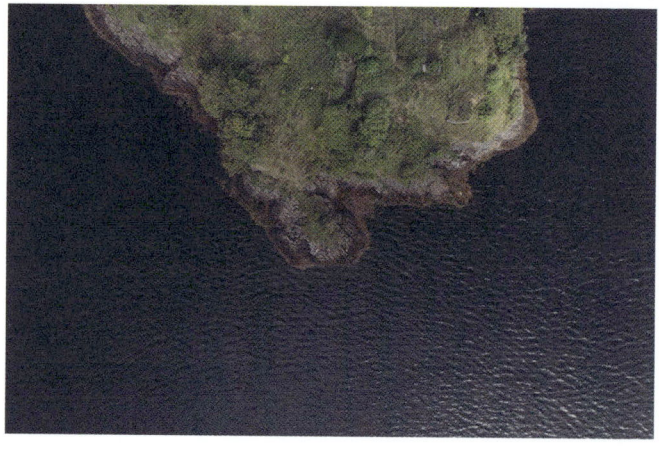

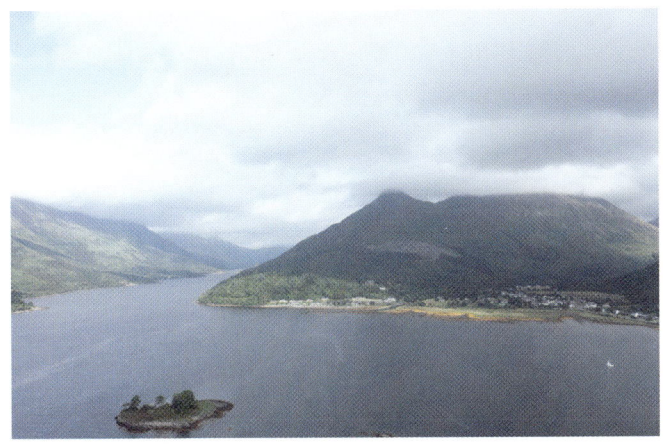

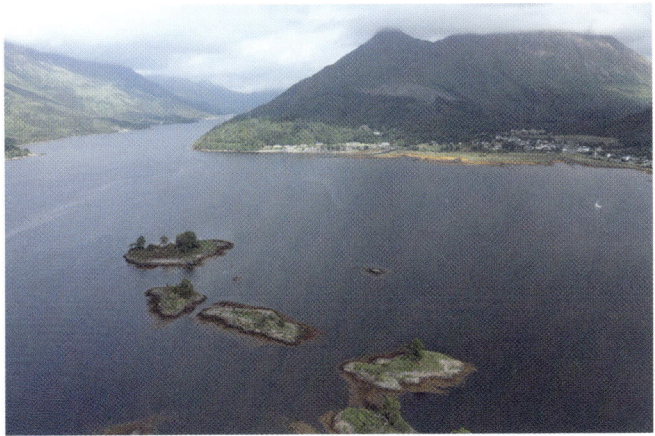

◀ ▲ *The five source images for the vertorama. Note how the lowest image is a straight vertical shot and the highest includes some interesting background and some sky.*

POST-PROCESSING

You will probably end up with three to five images—these can be in Jpeg or Raw format. In your photo editor of choice, blend them into one long, thin image. The exact technique will vary according to your software. In Photoshop, go to File>Automate>Photomerge.

ASSIGNMENT
18

TIPS

- Steeply sloping beaches will have one line of breakers, whereas more gently shelving beaches will have a wide surf zone. Go for a steep beach if you want powerful waves with the beach in shot. A wide surf zone can also make for great abstract wave shots.

- If the waves are large, avoid hovering too low over the water so your drone doesn't get a lethal saltwater dousing.

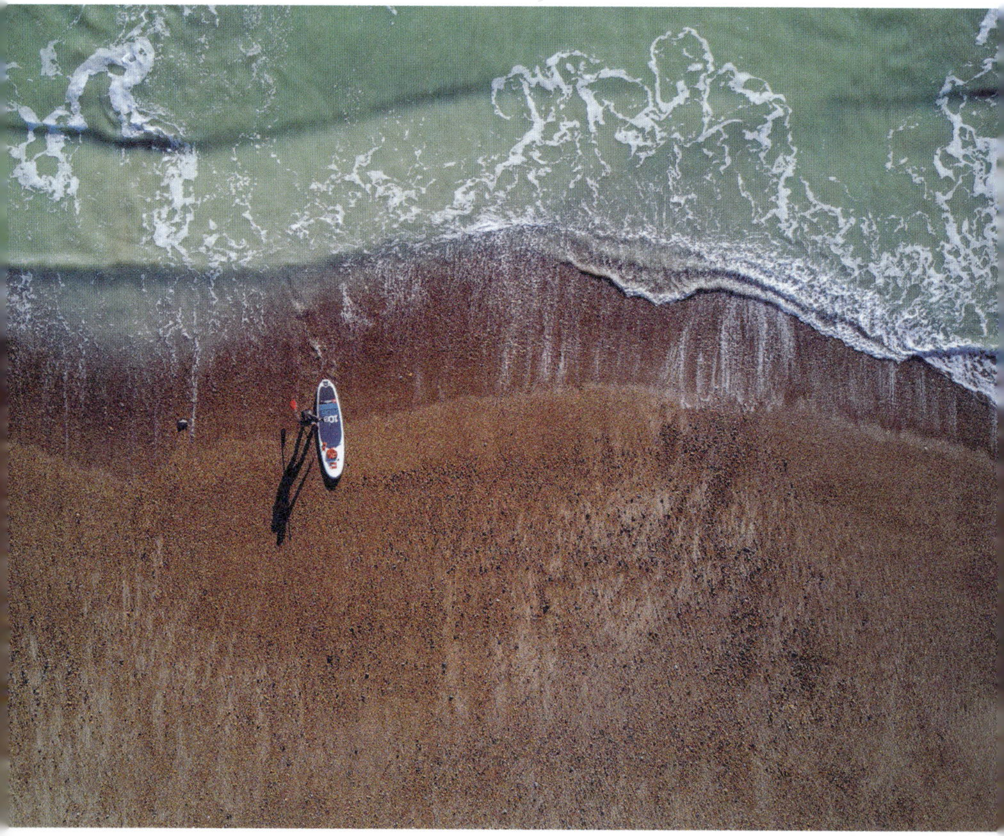

BREAKING WAVES

Waves breaking on or close to the shore can create great shapes and textures. Your assignment is to capture these shapes and textures with your drone, creating an interesting image of ocean meeting land. You may choose to make them the main compositional element or just part of the wider picture. The fact that a breaking wave produces white foam will draw the eye, so pay attention to any interesting shoreline features that may give the wave a particular curve. A top-down shot often gives an interesting perspective to shots of waves, but you may find other angles that also work well. Single waves breaking onto steeper shores can produce nice delineations between sea and land.

I like to get the drone in the air and arrange the compositional elements as I want them, perhaps placing the shoreline on a Rule-of-Thirds grid line, down the middle of the frame or on a diagonal. Once the elements are in place, it's a question of shooting plenty of shots until you get one where a wave breaks just right. As always, avoid hovering over crowds of people and be mindful of privacy concerns. If there is a lot of white water in the shot, be careful not to overexpose the highlights, perhaps by dialing in some negative exposure compensation.

POST-PROCESSING

A subtle boost to clarity or texture can often enhance the detail in the breaking waves. If the water has a dull or unattractive hue, play with the colors, perhaps boosting the greens or blues.

ASSIGNMENT JOURNAL

◀ *The breaking wave makes a nice line between ocean and land, emphasizing the transition from one element to another. The paddle boarder adds a point of human interest.*

ASSIGNMENT

19

TIPS

- Always take extra care near cliffs or drops, especially when distracted by a screen.

- If your drone features a Point of Interest intelligent flight mode, you may be able to extract a good still frame from the video.

- If you're capturing a tightly framed shot, double-check your focus. If you're focusing manually, it may need tweaking when you get close to your subject.

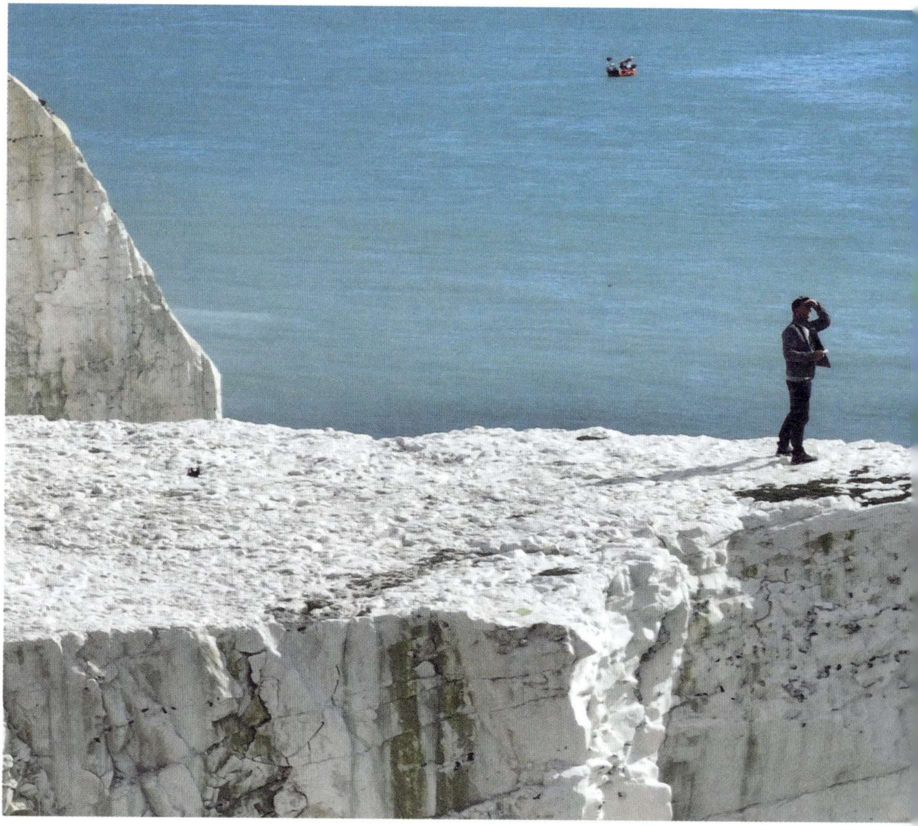

LONE FIGURE

We've probably all watched a movie or TV series featuring a scene in which the camera circles the hero standing on a spectacular mountain or beach. Well, this is your chance to photograph a lone figure in an equally dramatic setting.

Look for a location where the figure stands out against the background. A tighter lens or zoom function can add drama by compressing the image (making the backdrop appear larger). You could even be the hero and shoot a self-portrait—just remember to strike a bold pose and don't be looking at your screen when you take the photo.

Try different compositions with the drone at different altitudes. Depending on the background, you might want a high or low angle, and remember you can easily move around 360° so experiment with the angle of the light—maybe you can include an epic sunset as the background.

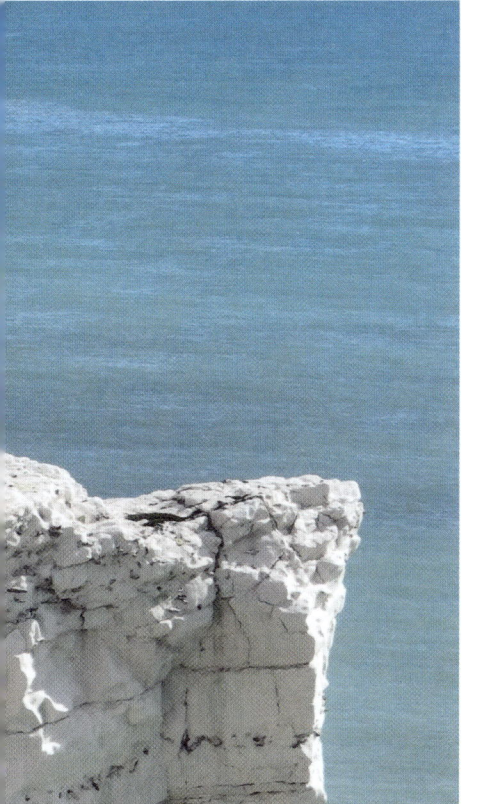

ASSIGNMENT JOURNAL

_____

_____

_____

_____

_____

_____

_____

◀ *The figure on the chalk cliffs stands out well against the blue of the ocean. This was only achievable using the elevated perspective provided by the drone.*

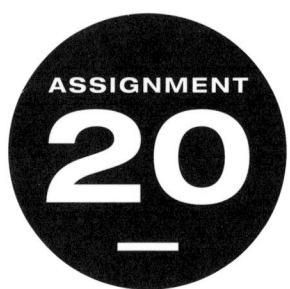

ASSIGNMENT
20

TIPS

- Never fly close to nervous animals, particularly horses, as they are easily spooked and can harm themselves.

- Multiple shadows will all fall in the same direction, so think about their orientation relative to the frame to achieve the most pleasing composition. Diagonal shadows can work well, but the best results will depend on the rest of your composition, so definitely experiment with angles.

SHADOW ABSTRACTS

When shooting top-down drone images, the subject is often hard to recognize from an unfamiliar angle, so for this assignment, you're going to use shadows to reveal their identity. Animals, people, and trees can all make good subject matter for this type of shot because of their easily recognizable silhouettes.

It's worth remembering that if the sun is at around 45° above the horizon, shadows will be roughly in proportion. A lower angle will give an elongated shadow whereas a higher angle will give a foreshortened angle, so plan your shoot with that in mind. You'll want full sun to achieve the sharpest shadows—a slightly overcast or hazy sky will make the shadows softer and less distinct.

Choose a surface that is relatively uniform and preferably a light tone for the best shadow contrast. In terms of exposure, you should be fine using automatic settings. If there's much movement in the shot, ensure your shutter speed is 1/500 sec. or above, which shouldn't be a problem in full sun. If you're shooting a person, ask them to change their pose until you have the most striking shadow.

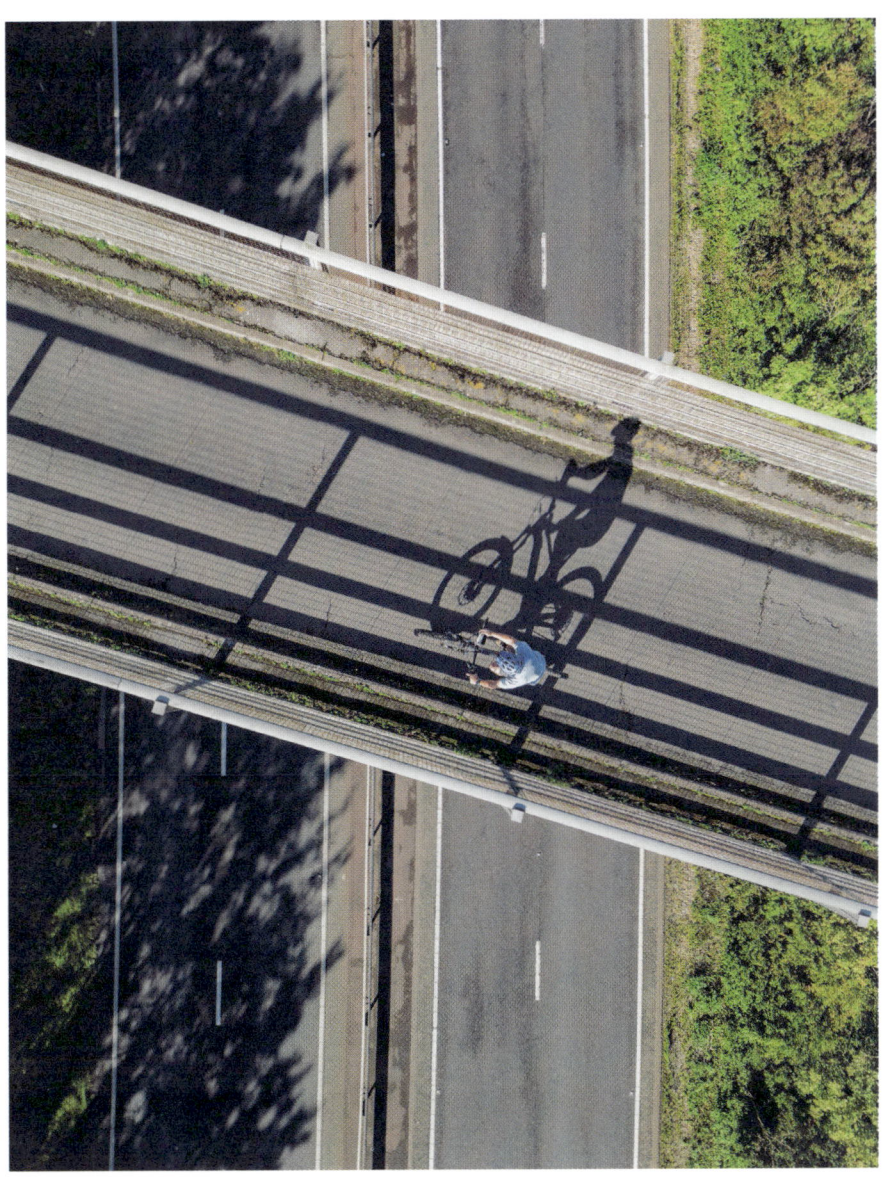

▲ *Bicycles make particularly compelling subjects for shadow work. I also used the roads and the shadows of the fence as compositional elements.*

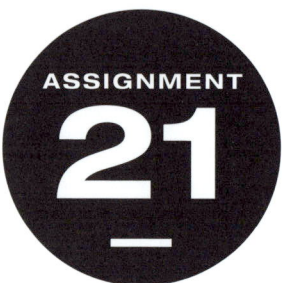

ASSIGNMENT
21

TIPS

- Consult tide tables if the river is tidal. High tide will give more water, while at low tide you may get large, exposed areas of mud.

- Be aware of any wildlife or nature reserves so as not to disturb any bird-feeding or nesting areas.

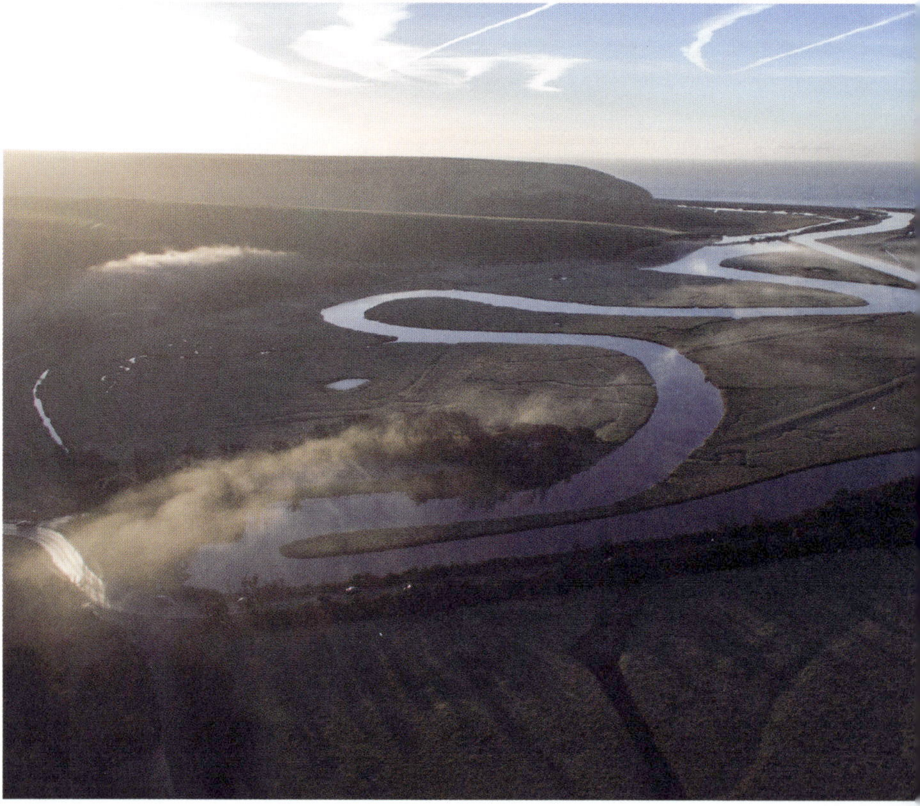

WINDING RIVERS

Rivers snake their way through the landscape in a way that can only truly be appreciated from the air, making them perfect subjects for drone photography. Your assignment is to shoot a landscape image in which a river provides a curvaceous focal point. You may be able to use local knowledge to find good locations close to home or satellite imagery to find places where a river makes interesting shapes. Once you arrive at your location, it may help to get the drone up good and high to scout the areas that show the most promise. For your final composition, think about emphasizing any interesting features of the river such as meandering curves or feeder channels.

You may find that to get the water to stand out against darker land, you need to get some nice sky reflections, so returning at a different time of day might be a good option. If the river is tidal, you might need to wait until the water level changes to optimize the composition. As well as the shape of the river itself, any features on the riverbank can add or detract from your composition so think carefully about what you include or exclude. Boats, buildings, and trees might add interest.

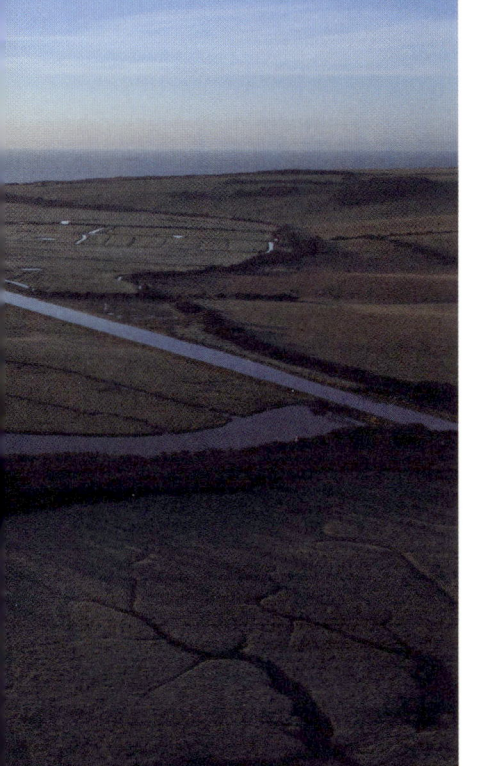

ASSIGNMENT JOURNAL

_____

_____

_____

_____

_____

_____

_____

◀ *Patches of morning mist add to the atmosphere of this winter scene. I could have shot an HDR image and avoided the slightly overexposed area of sky on the left.*

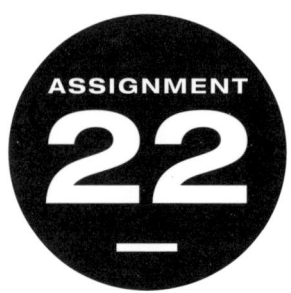

ASSIGNMENT
22

TIPS

- Try keeping the drone below the canopy height and get shots from close to the tree branches. These can be abstract shots that give you a slightly different perspective than the one you get with your feet planted on the ground.

- Roads make a good feature to shoot if they traverse a dense forest.

LOST IN THE FOREST

When viewed from above, forests and woods look very different to the familiar view we get when immersed in one. Your assignment is to take a drone photograph of a forest using the elevated perspective to emphasize the variety or uniformity of the forest, and capture the striking textures, colors, and patterns of the treetops.

Your first task is to find a safe takeoff and landing spot. This can be problematic if you're in the middle of dense vegetation, so it's best to choose either a large clearing or a spot on the edge of the forest that will allow you to maintain a visual line of sight with your drone. Bear in mind that leaves are very good at interfering in the radio transmission, so if trees come between you and your drone you could lose control link and/or video transmission. If the Return to Home (RTH) feature is initiated, you need to make sure the RTH altitude is well above treetop height.

Provided you can keep a line of sight to your drone, try taking the drone as high as you are allowed. Can you spot any areas of interest in the forest? You may find you need to descend to get a closer perspective on the area but might then lose visual contact with the drone. If this is the case, you should return to your takeoff spot and see if you can reset your takeoff to a better vantage point.

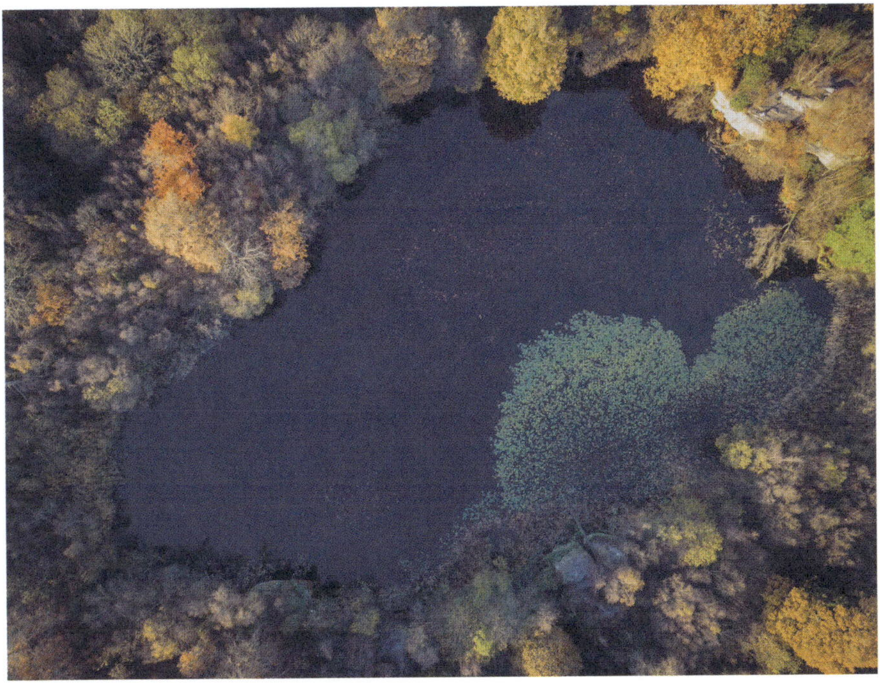

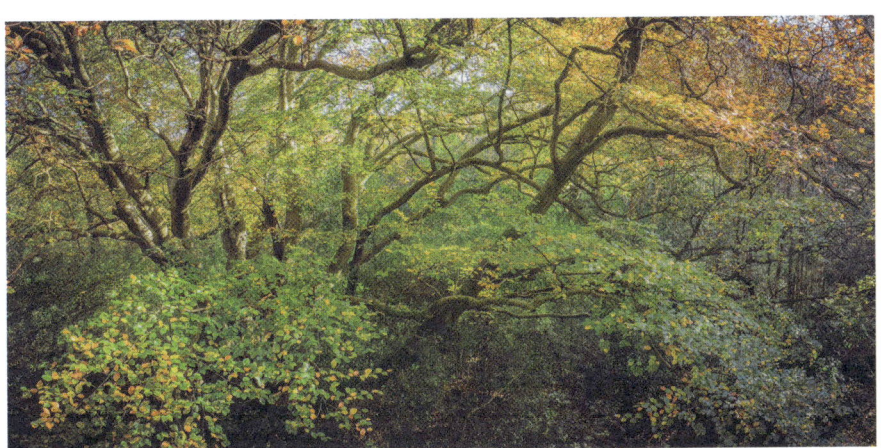

▲ Different species of trees surround a forest lake, giving a variety of colors and shapes.

▲ This image was taken from an altitude of only 26ft (8m), very close to the canopy of a beech tree. The backlit leaves are beginning to turn autumnal, adding to the palette.

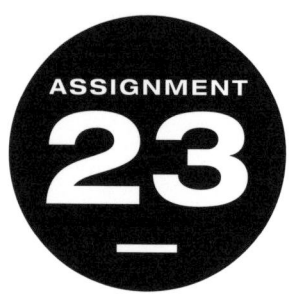

ASSIGNMENT
23

TIPS

- Buildings, cars, and trains are all subjects that look good as miniatures.

- Shoot at an angle that gives a relatively large amount of depth in the image. You may not need to be too high, but you do need a good range of distances between foreground and background.

MINIATURE EFFECT

You've probably seen real-world shots that look like miniature models. They are sometimes known as tilt-shift shots because the purest way of taking them is using a tilt-shift lens on a DSLR or mirrorless camera. These lenses tilt the plane of focus relative to the sensor plane, so that only a thin sliver of the image is in focus. However, unless you own a heavy lift drone and gimbal, you'll struggle to get such images in camera from the air. But all is not lost—once you have your image, it's a relatively quick and simple process to add a gradient blur and make some basic adjustments with your image-editing software to achieve a similar effect.

Your assignment is to take a drone photograph and modify it using a miniature "tilt-shift" effect. Urban, suburban, and industrial scenes are often most effective, and make sure you place your main subject somewhere in the central part of your frame. Once you've taken your image and processed it, assess whether the tilt-shift effect has been successful. Is it a convincing effect, or is there anything you'd do differently next time?

▶ *I liked the idea of a huge truck appearing like a child's toy. The opportunity arose when I found an aggregate depot surrounded by open land—ideal for drone flying.*

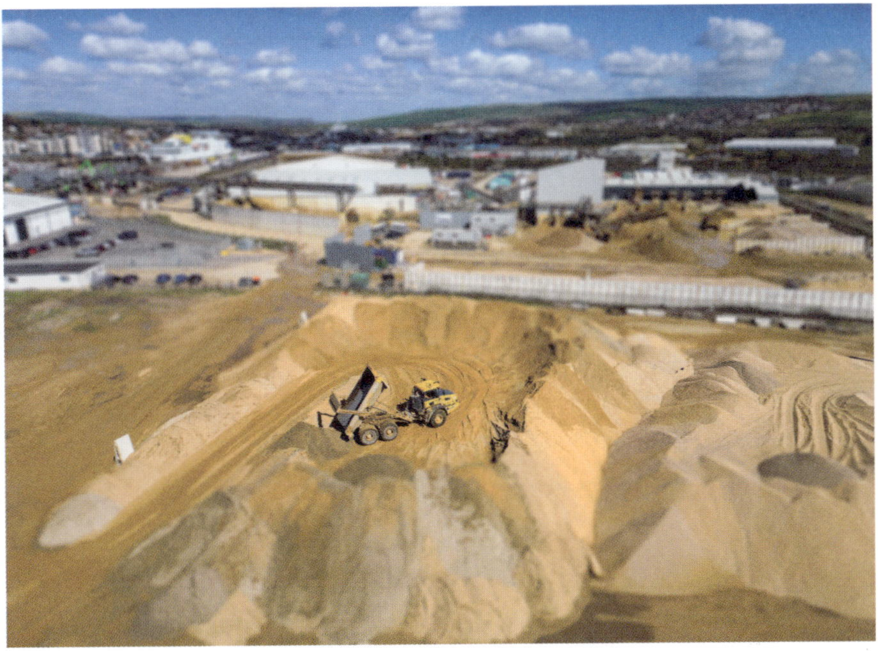

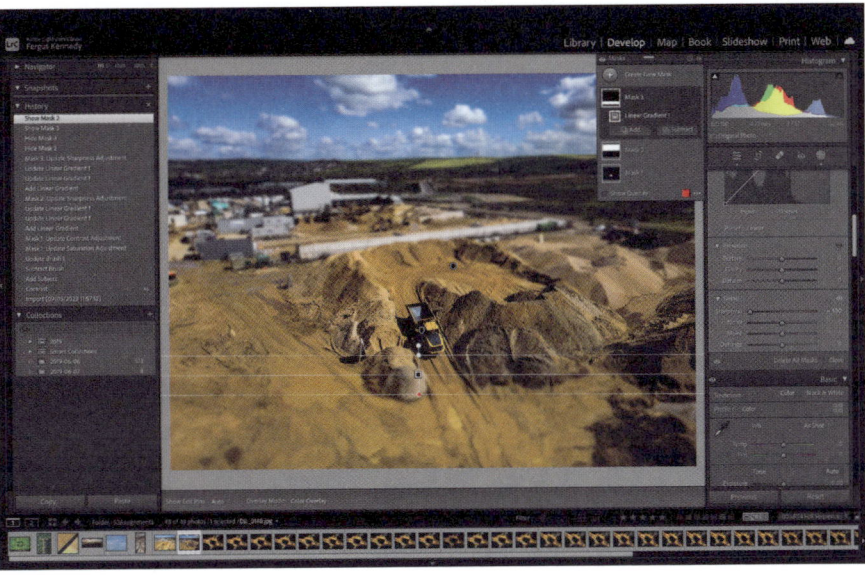

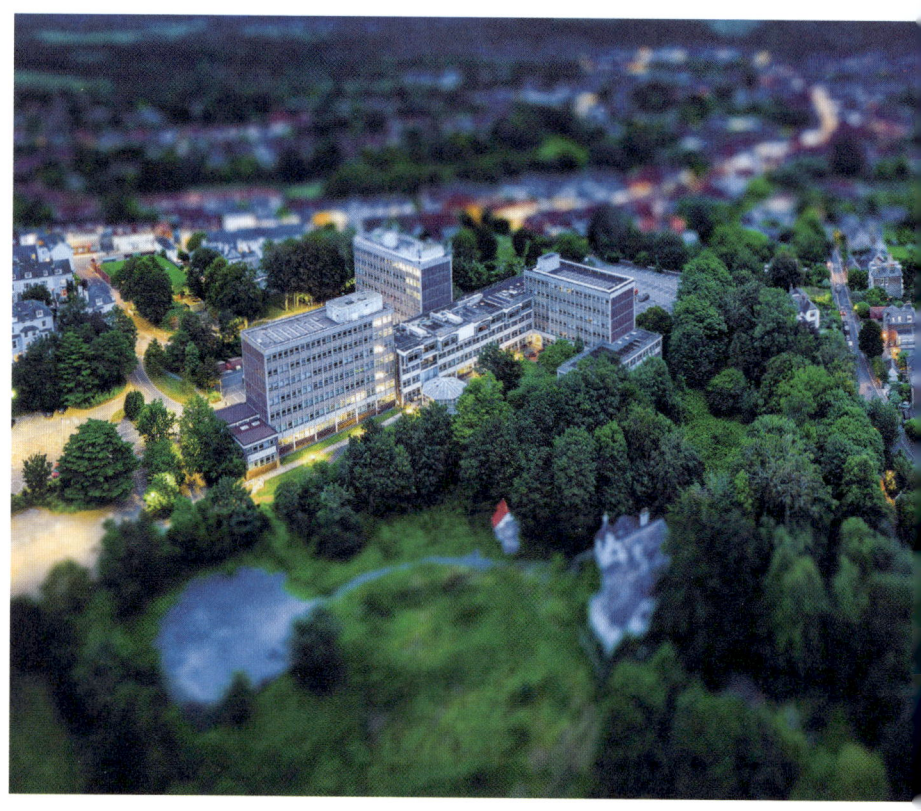

POST-PROCESSING

Use two linear gradient filters and add a Gaussian blur effect to each, leaving a narrow strip of sharp focus between the two. Play with the angles and the transition of the gradient to get the best effect. The sharp strip is often horizontal, but you can also try various degrees of diagonal (see screenshot). Software such as Adobe Photoshop has a fully automated Tilt Shift feature under the Filter menu, which allows you to adjust the strength and angle of the effect. Upping the contrast, dehaze, and saturation will often enhance the miniature effect, making it look more like a toy world.

ASSIGNMENT JOURNAL

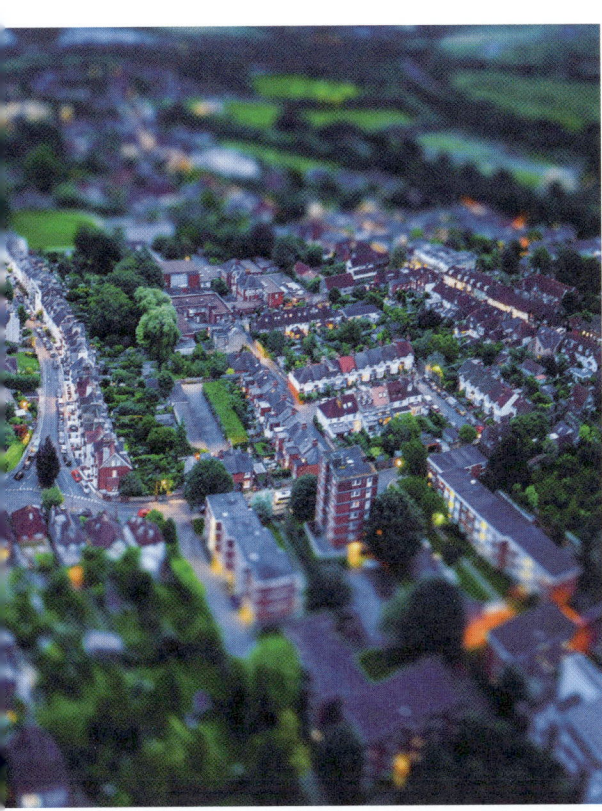

◄ *These office blocks with surrounding housing and park areas looked great as miniatures.*

▼ *An Adobe Photoshop screenshot showing the Tilt Shift filter in place.*

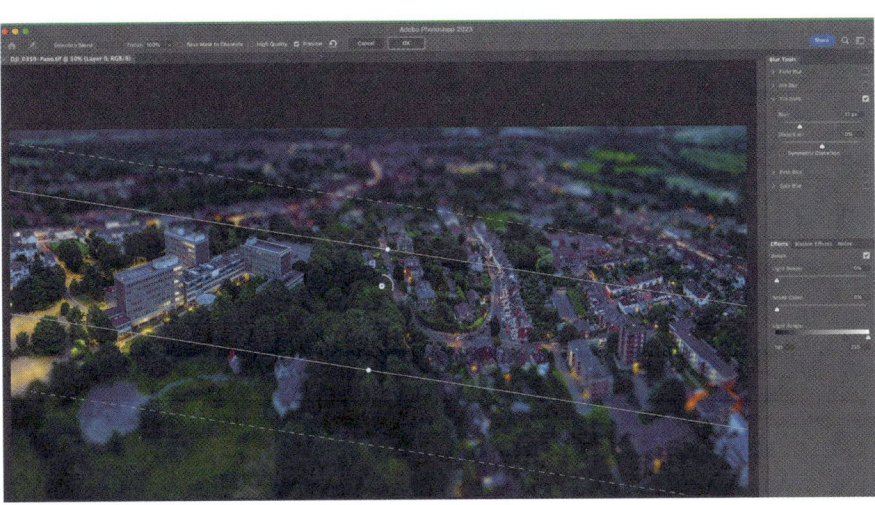

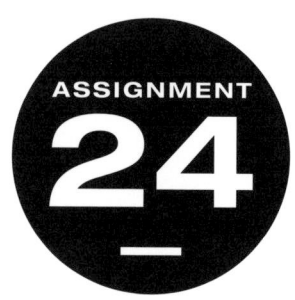

ASSIGNMENT

24

TIPS

- Choose a day with light winds to ensure the drone can maintain its position long enough to shoot the HDR sequence.

- If you have the option, shoot in Raw to get the most out of the files—the extra data allows you to make bigger changes in the edit without affecting image quality.

- Most software has an HDR setting that will automatically align and blend two or more shots. Just take care not to overdo the effect, as the results can look artificial.

HIGH DYNAMIC RANGE

High dynamic range (HDR) is a technique that blends two or more shots taken at different exposures to produce a single image with plenty of detail in both the shadow and highlight areas. Your assignment is to shoot and process an HDR drone image that plays to the strengths of this technique.

HDR is best used when the sky is much brighter than the land or foreground elements, for instance after sunset or before sunrise. During the shooting phase, if you have a bright sky but no detail in the land, this is the perfect time to use HDR.

Depending on the model, your drone may have a built-in HDR mode, where it will shoot three or more shots and blend them in camera. If not, you still have several options. Auto Exposure Bracketing mode allows you to shoot three or more shots in rapid succession at a predetermined exposure spacing (for example, 1 stop under, correct exposure, 1 stop over). Alternatively, use exposure compensation to achieve the same bracketing sequence. Make sure you don't move the drone between shots.

▶ *The three source images at –2 EV, 0 EV, and +2 EV.*

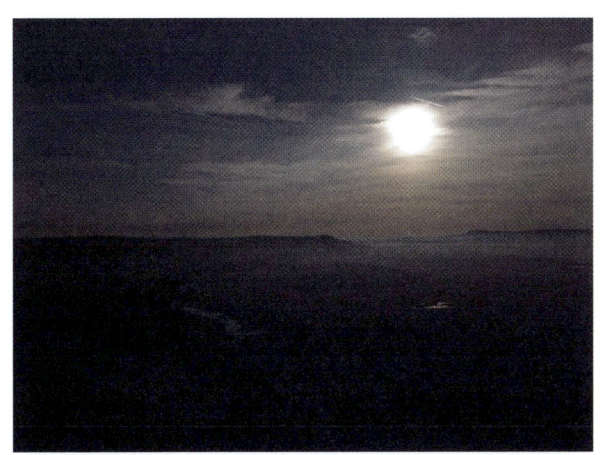

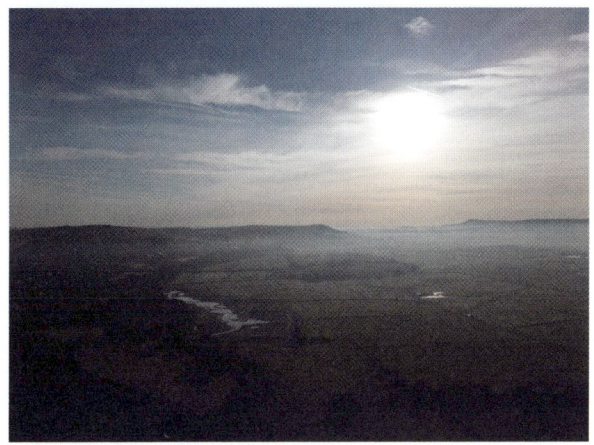

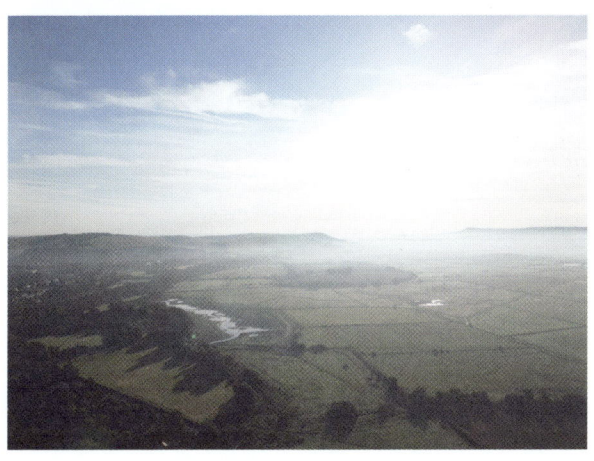

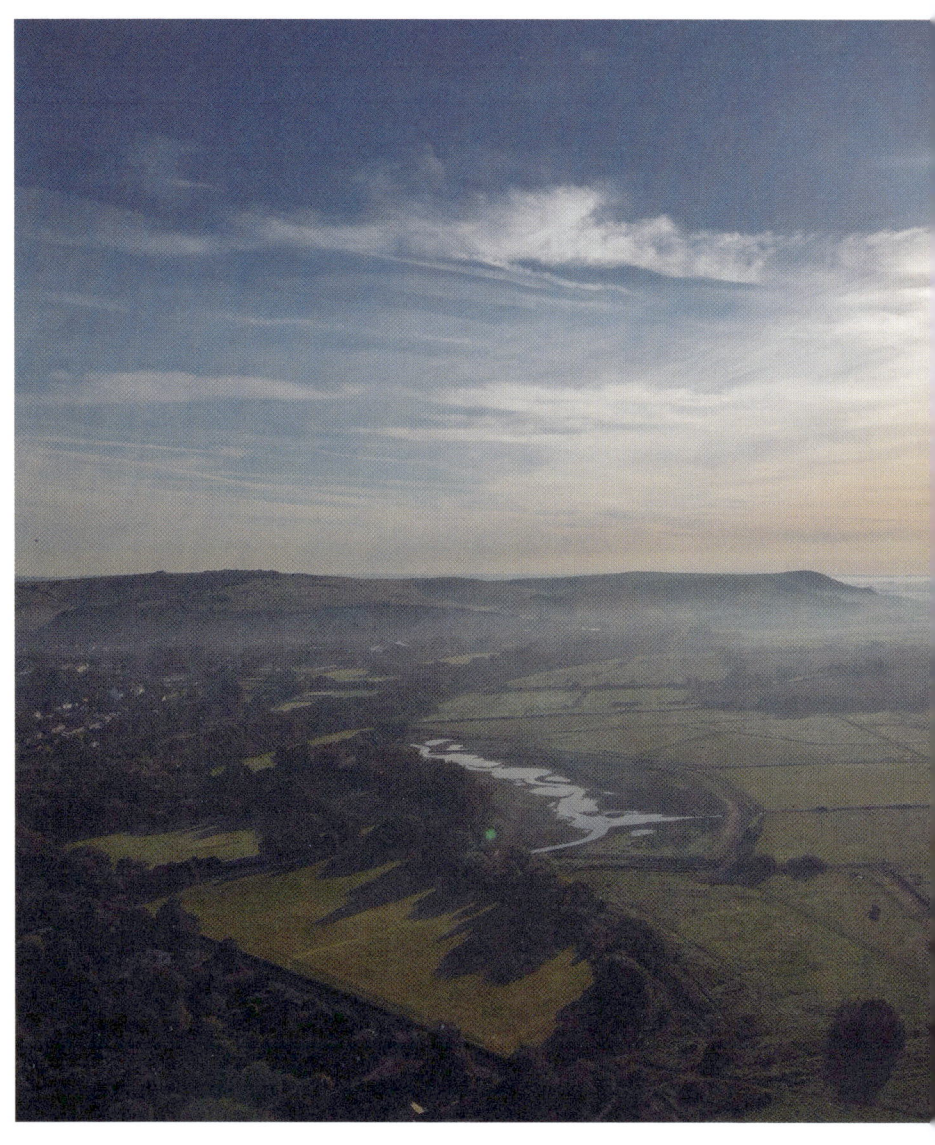

▲ *The blended result with better shadow and highlight detail.*

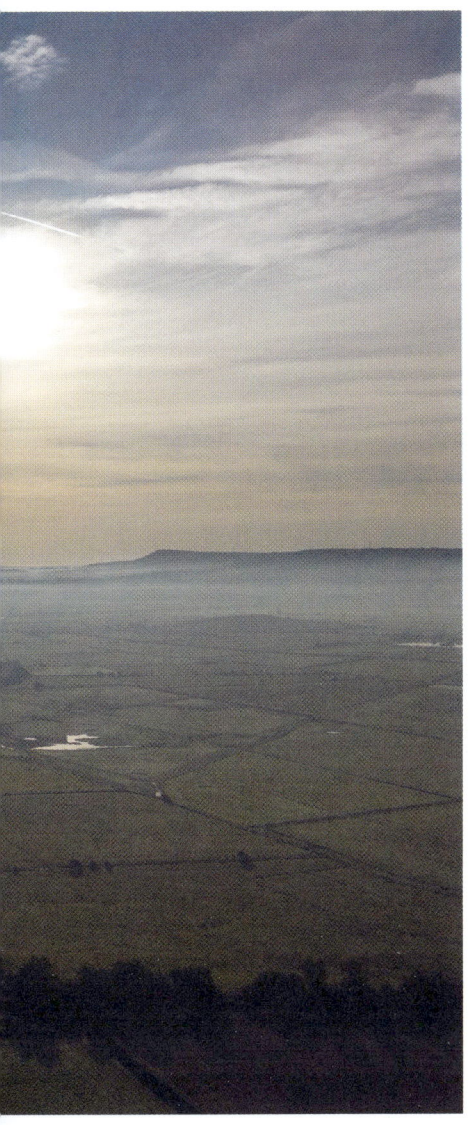

ASSIGNMENT JOURNAL

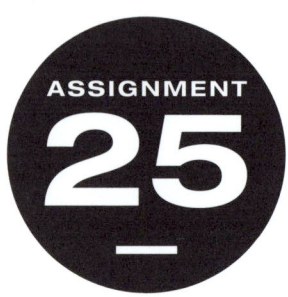

ASSIGNMENT
25

TIPS

- Get to know the times of different farm activities in your area—seed-drilling, harvesting, and plowing all use different vehicles or trailers.

- Don't trespass. If in doubt, ask the landowner for permission.

▶ *A close-up of a combine harvester, highlighting the lines and textures.*

▼ *I liked the way the tracks circled the oak tree in the field, so for another shot I composed the scene and waited until the combine harvester moved into the frame.*

DOWN ON THE FARM

Since the advent of automated, GPS-controlled farm vehicles, there are often very neat, geometric lines in farmers' fields. For this assignment, you will be focusing on these lines and how they are formed, using your drone's aerial perspective to include both interesting patterns and farm vehicles plowing, harvesting, or planting crops.

I've had good results with photographing plowing, when flocks of gulls follow the tractor, and combine harvesters in wheat fields. If you can find a friendly farmer, they may have ideas for what would look good, and you could thank them with a nice set of prints.

If you're photographing moving farm vehicles, try to match their speed and direction. Once you are doing this competently, get creative and experiment with different angles and light directions, all while keeping the vehicle nicely framed. If you are going to fly close to the vehicle, you should talk to the farmer first, so the drone isn't an unwelcome distraction.

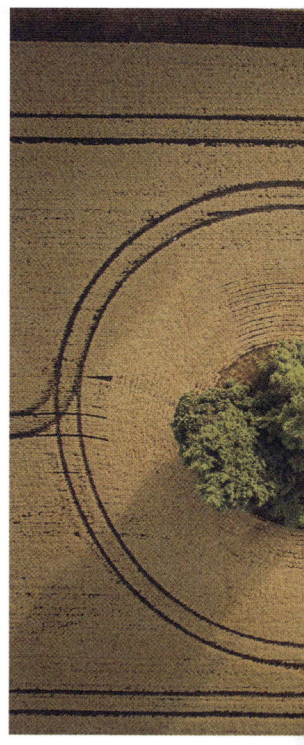

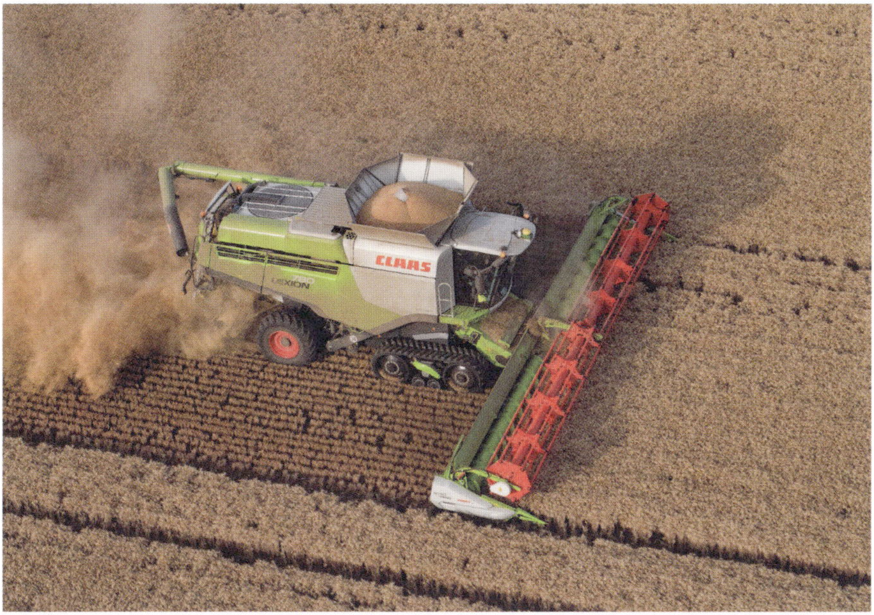
CLAAS

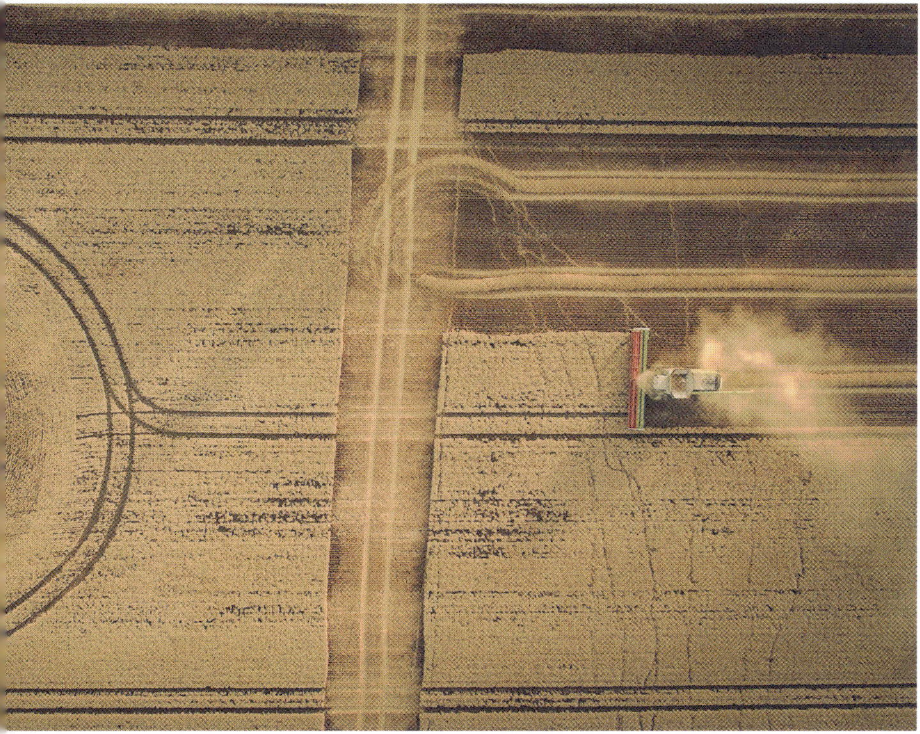

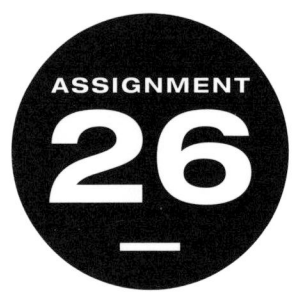

ASSIGNMENT

26

TIPS

- For best results, choose a windless day. Wind will introduce drone movement, which could affect the alignment of the images.

- Choose an area with visual interest directly below the drone and avoid large areas of water, as they are hard to stitch.

- Ensure you have plenty of flight time left in the battery before starting, as it can take several minutes to acquire all the source photographs.

- Start the panorama with the drone facing the sun or the brightest part of the sky, so that the exposure is appropriate for that area and not overexposed.

LITTLE PLANET

Technically known as stereographic projections of 360°x180° panoramas, "little planet" images are created by stitching together several images and remapping them so that the scene looks like a small planet. Your assignment is to create your own "little planet" image that transforms a familiar landscape into a 360° sphere.

Depending on which model of drone you have, the shooting and stitching may be done entirely automatically—look for a 360° sphere panorama mode or similar—or you may need to shoot and stitch manually. You may also have the option to save the source images as Raw files as well as the final panorama, which is worth doing in case the in-drone stitching doesn't work out.

If you don't have the automated option, you will need to manually shoot columns and rows of images, each overlapping by 40 percent. Repeat until you have the whole sphere covered (you may end up with over 30 images).

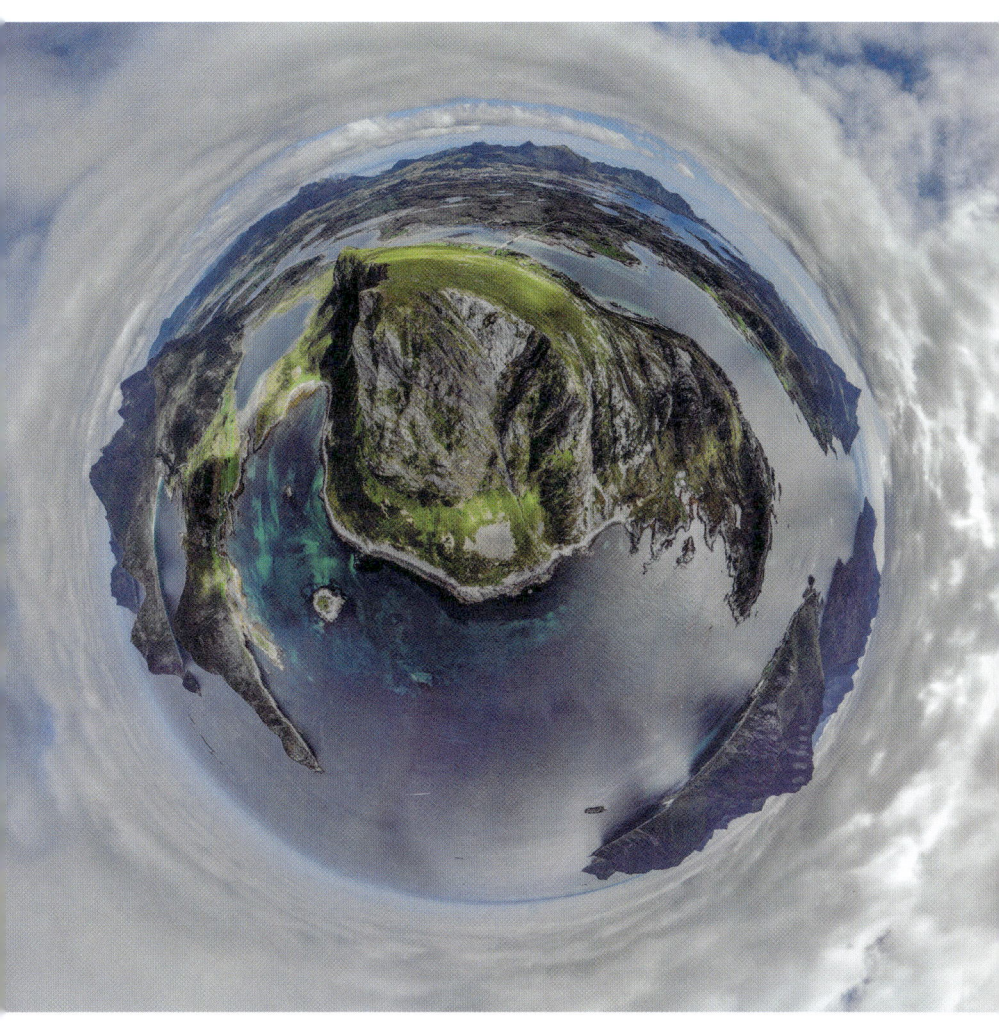

▲ The green landscape and blue sea of Norway make this image look like a miniature version of Earth. The mountainous scenery adds interest.

POST-PROCESSING

If your drone has an automated 360º sphere panorama option, you'll simply need to make the usual minor adjustments during post-processing. If you manually shot the panorama, stitch the source images together in your photo editor of choice, choosing first equirectangular panorama, then stereographic projection.

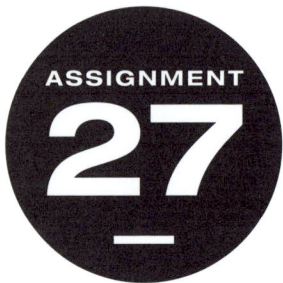

ASSIGNMENT
27

TIPS

- Retain the original stills for finer processing options. You can edit the Raw files or even Jpegs more successfully than a video file, and later compile them into a video file. Most video-editing programs can do this.

- The best results can be had by using manual exposure.

- Always check you have sufficient battery capacity left to complete the flight.

- Specify a very slow flight speed, or the drone will soon get too far away from you.

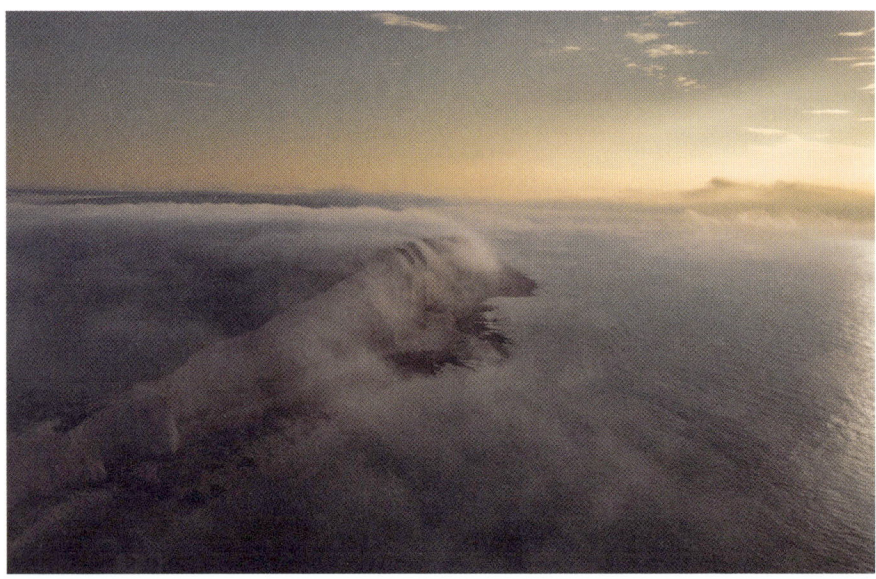

HYPERLAPSE

A timelapse is a static video clip in which minutes or hours are compressed into a few seconds. A hyperlapse is a timelapse in which the camera moves during the clip.

A hyperlapse takes planning and preparation, so if this is your first time, get a feel for it by first shooting a timelapse from your drone. Suitable subjects might include fog, traffic on roads, or clouds moving by. The slower the action, the longer the interval you can use between shots. For instance, if shooting slow-moving clouds, you might try an 8 or 10-sec. interval, but if shooting pedestrians or traffic, a 1 or 2-sec. interval would be more appropriate.

Most modern drones feature a hyperlapse mode that allows you to specify the interval, start, and stop positions, and even waypoints. As a slightly simpler option, you can just specify the direction of flight and camera angle and leave it running until your battery starts to get low or you are approaching the limits of your safe-flying range. Some drones will then automatically produce the time-lapse video.

Those with older models will need to set the drone to take a photo every second or so, then fly at a very low but constant speed in a fixed direction. You can then use software such as Adobe Premiere Pro or Microsoft Time Lapse Creator to compile the sequence of still photos into the finished hyperlapse video.

ASSIGNMENT JOURNAL

_____   _____

_____   _____

_____   _____

_____   _____

_____   _____

_____   _____

◄ *Hyperlapsed fog can take on a liquid-like motion, as was the case on this atmospheric morning on the coast.*

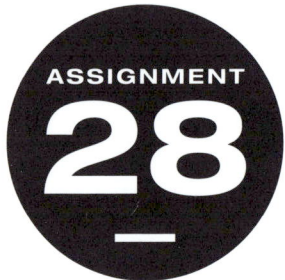

ASSIGNMENT
28

TIPS

• Use manual exposure to avoid unwanted automatic adjustments as the average brightness changes during the move.

• Practice by getting your start and end frames exactly as you want them first, then work on the transition between the two.

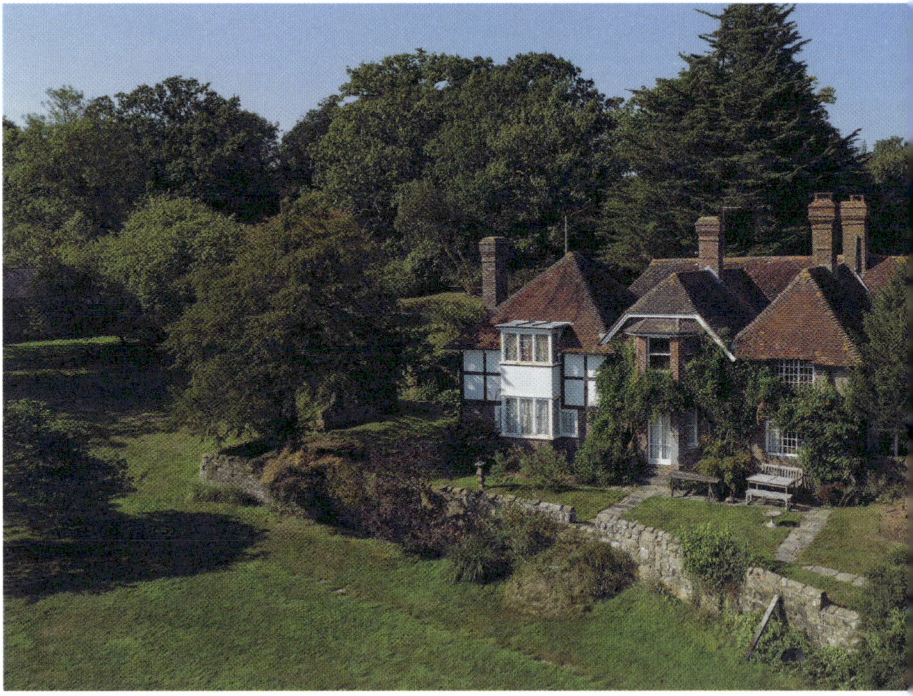

THE BIG REVEAL

In film and television, a "reveal" is a shot where the main subject is revealed after being out of shot or obscured by another object. It can be a great way of adding drama and interest to a shot. Your assignment is to produce a video clip that reveals your subject in a creative way.

There are many ways to reveal a subject. A favorite might be to fly past a tree, so that the tree is between the drone and the subject, and the tree then sweeps across the frame from right to left (or vice versa) to reveal a stunning house and garden. Or it might involve the drone ascending over a rise in the landscape revealing a person. It could even be a tilt up to reveal a magnificent landscape as the drone travels fast and low over the ground.

It's a simple concept but it can be tricky to execute smoothly, so you may need several attempts to nail it. Give some consideration to how long you want the clip to be—is it a slow reveal or a faster, more dynamic reveal? As you get more confident, you can try more complicated camera moves, for instance descending diagonally while tilting the camera up. This sort of "compound" move can add dynamism.

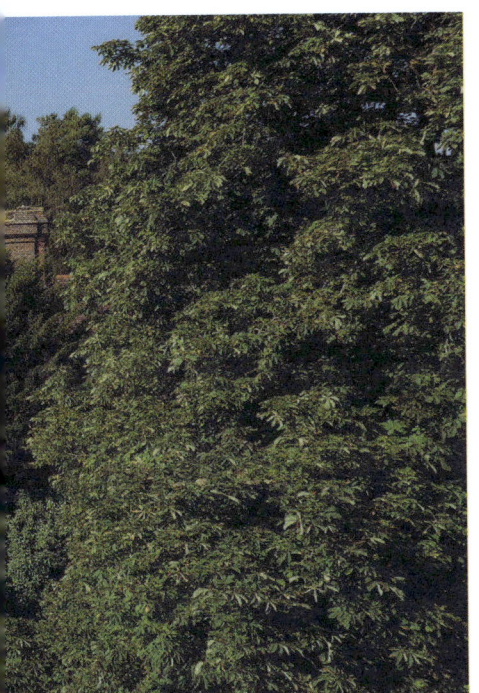

◀ *Trees can make great foregrounds for a reveal of a house, as the drone moves around the obstruction.*

ASSIGNMENT JOURNAL

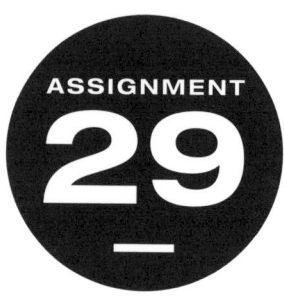

ASSIGNMENT 29

TIPS

- Set your shutter speed to twice the frame rate. So, if you're shooting at 100 fps, use a shutter speed of 1/200 sec.

- If you're feeling adventurous, try a "speed ramp" in your editing software. This is when the video transitions from normal speed to slow motion for an eye-catching effect.

▶ *A gravity-defying mountain biker jumping in the forest makes a great subject for a slow-motion video.*

ASSIGNMENT JOURNAL

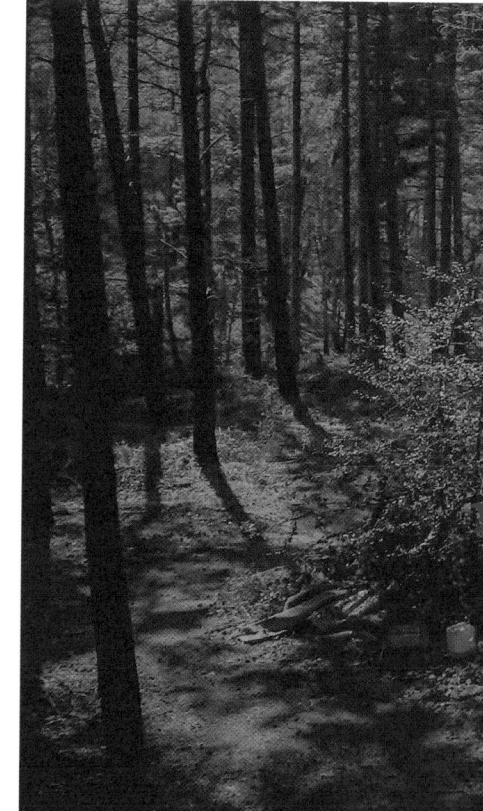

SLOOOOW MOTION

Many modern drones feature slow-motion video modes. Video is usually shot at 24, 25, or 30 frames per second (fps). If you select a faster frame rate (48, 50, or 60 fps), you can halve the playback speed and still get smooth video. Some drones even offer frame rates of up to 120 fps, allowing you to slow down the video by four times.

Subject selection is key for this technique, as you need some elements in the shot that play to its strengths. So, a car splashing through water, a bike jumping, waves crashing on the beach, or people running all make good subjects.

Remember that if the action is fast, it'll be trickier to catch the key moments, but you may only need a few seconds of action if you're going to slow it down. Depending on your drone, it may slow down the footage in camera (this is often the case with 100 or 120 fps footage), or you may need to do it in your video-editing software.

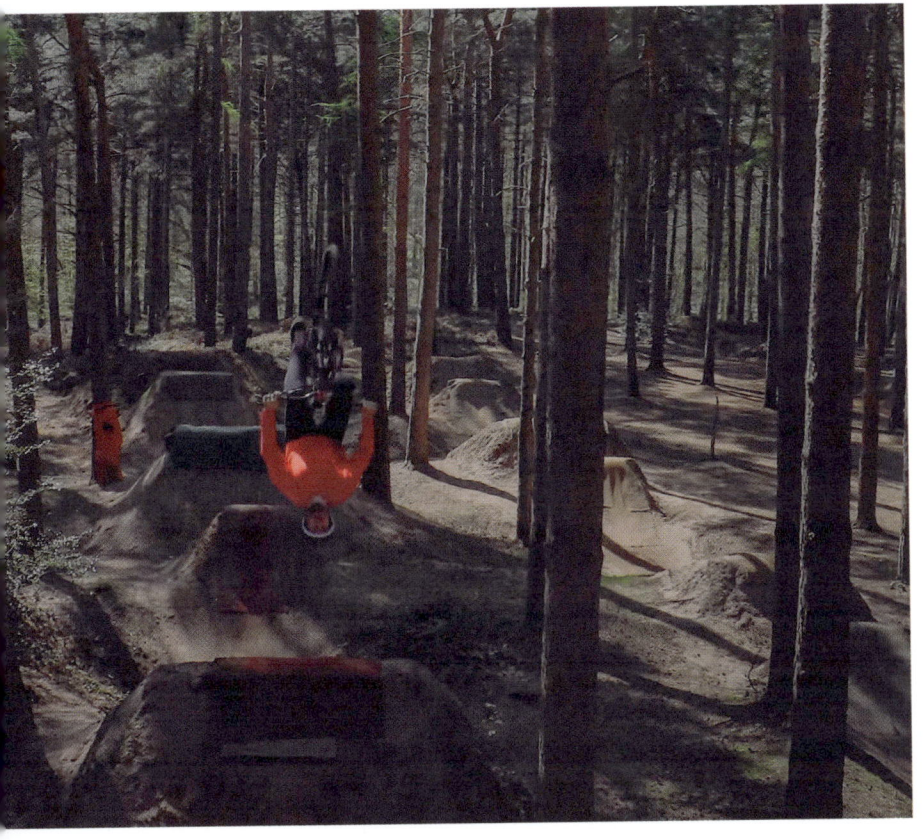

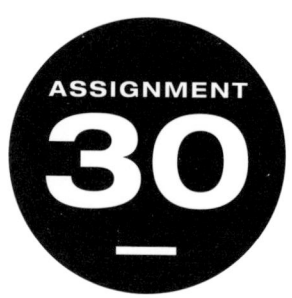

ASSIGNMENT

30

TIPS

- Err on the side of underexposure to avoid blowing out any highlights in the sky.

- Don't give up too soon—a small gap in the clouds can sometimes produce epic colors, if only for a few minutes.

- You may not need to position the drone very high for the best results. For instance, you might want a foreground feature silhouetted, in which case you would want to stay relatively low. Or you might want to exclude foreground obstructions, in which case you'd fly a bit higher.

SUNSETS AND SUNRISES

You may think that sunsets and sunrises are a subject best shot from ground level, but drones offer some great advantages for capturing those epic explosions of sky color. The problem with having your camera stuck at ground level is there are often obstructions blocking the view. The drone allows you to maneuver your camera in three dimensions until you've found a composition that combines the best foreground elements and that fabulous sky.

Your assignment is to use your drone to capture a fantastic sunrise or sunset. It pays to be prepared in advance, as you can identify the best spot for sunsets, then keep an eye on the weather forecast. The best sunset colors usually occur in a partially cloudy sky with a gap in the cloud on the western horizon. As the sun dips further below the horizon, it will illuminate the clouds from below with ever-changing hues. Distinct layers of cloud will give even more amazing results, each showing a different color. Luck plays a big part, so you'll need patience and persistence.

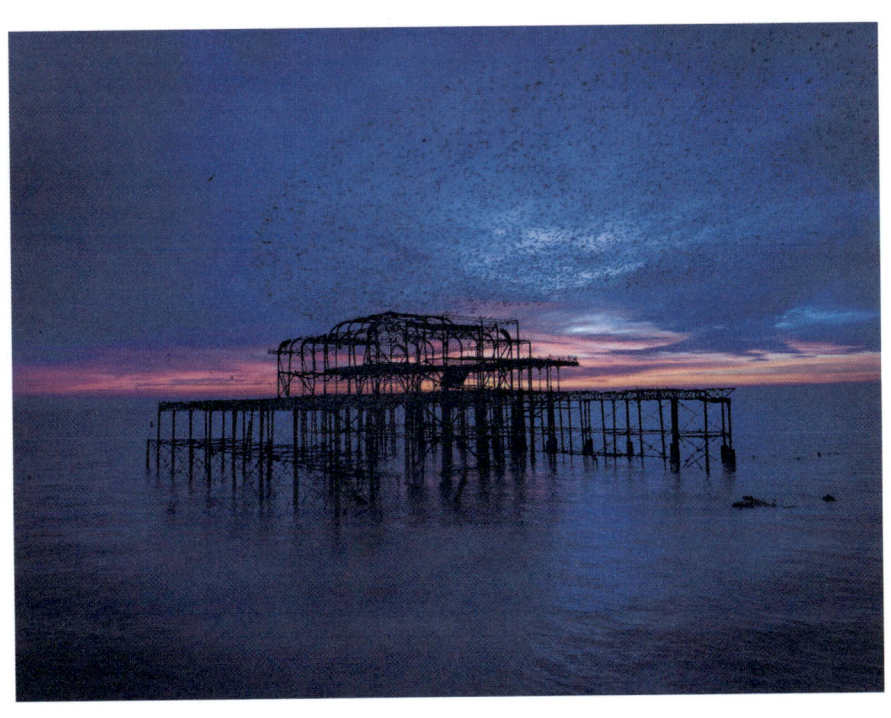

▲ *On this evening, the sky put on a mesmerizing and ever-changing display behind the remains of a pier.*

ASSIGNMENT JOURNAL

TIPS

- Try using a slower shutter speed (maybe with an ND filter) to accentuate the motion blur. Start at 1/frame rate.

- Avoid busy areas of woodland—early mornings may be a good option.

- Watch out for thin branches, as they're difficult to spot for both you and the drone's sensors.

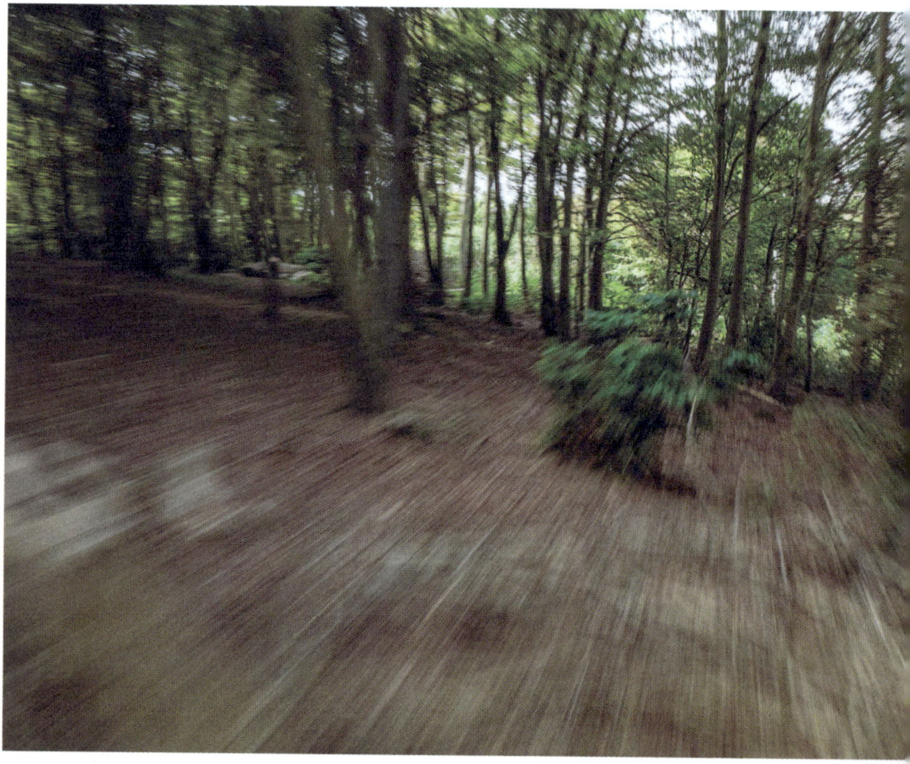

TREE DODGING

Wooded areas can make challenging environments in which to hone your flying skills, yet whizzing through trees can make for fantastic video clips—so long as you avoid collisions. Your assignment is to produce a fast-paced video clip in a forest setting.

If your drone has collision-avoidance sensors, it's best to activate these, at least to start with. Set them to "Bypass" so the drone will try to find a route around an obstacle rather than stopping dead. Once your flying skills are up to standard, you will get smoother results by disabling obstacle avoidance.

Keeping the drone relatively near to the ground can enhance the sense of speed and means that the drone is less likely to be badly damaged if you do suffer a collision with a tree. Using the widest focal length will also add to the drama. For this assignment, try flying with the camera facing forward, and then to the side. The side-looking video clip can give a great parallax effect, with the foreground trees speeding past at a much higher rate than those in the background.

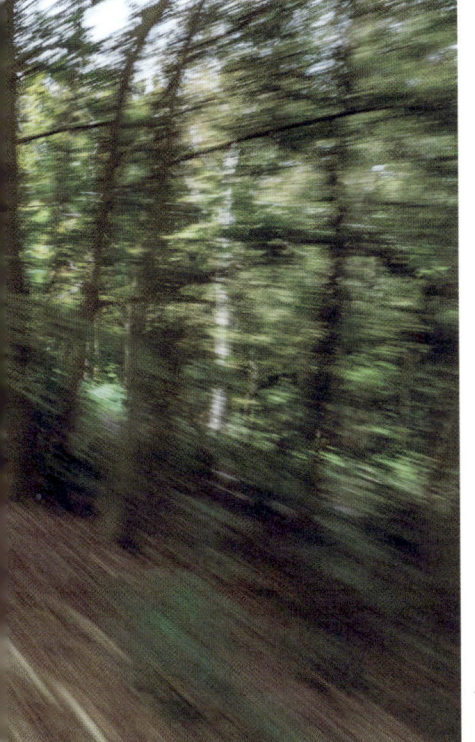

ASSIGNMENT JOURNAL

◄ *Flying close to the ground with a slower shutter speed accentuates the motion blur but can make collisions harder to avoid.*

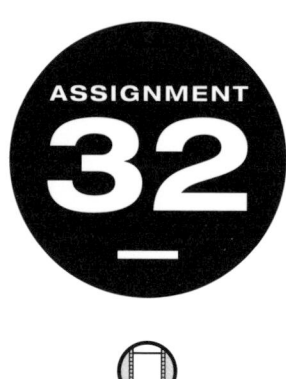

ASSIGNMENT

32

TIPS

- You need to be close enough to your subject for it to be recognized by the drone. If it's a human subject, we are talking 16–33ft (5–10m), perhaps a little further with vehicles.

- If you're filming yourself, don't be too distracted by the screen, as you need to keep your eyes on where you're walking, running, or cycling.

ACTIVE TRACK

Most modern drones can autonomously track a moving subject with almost spooky effectiveness. After taking off and identifying an appropriate subject, which could be a car, boat, cyclist, or runner, you simply draw a box around the subject on the touchscreen and choose your tracking mode—Spotlight, Parallel, or Trace. Spotlight allows you to fly freely while the drone automatically keeps the subject centered, Parallel tracks the subject from the side, moving parallel to the motion of the subject, and Trace follows a moving subject from behind, although newer drones often allow even more flexibility with 360° tracking options.

Your assignment is to produce a short video clip using this technique. Depending on your model of drone, the obstacle-avoidance system may not be fully functional—when it's flying sideways, it may not have side-looking sensors—so this is an assignment best practiced in an open environment.

Position the drone in a way that best highlights both your subject and any background features and be aware that the subject tracking will be most effective when the subject stands out visually against the background. If you want to be more creative, Spotlight mode (or similar) works by keeping the subject in the center of the frame while still allowing you to fly freely. Finally, if you have a drone that doesn't feature Active Track, all is not lost, as you can try tracking a moving subject manually—it's great practice for your flying skills.

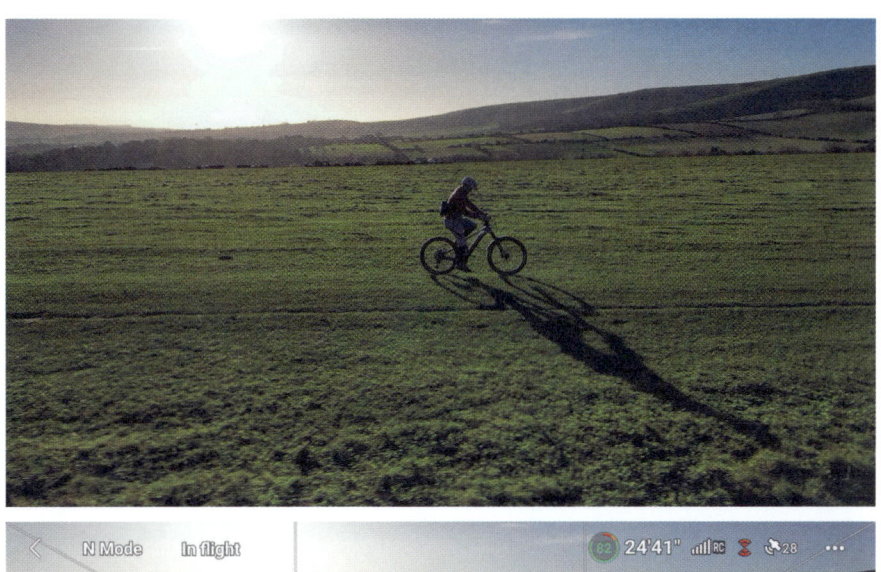

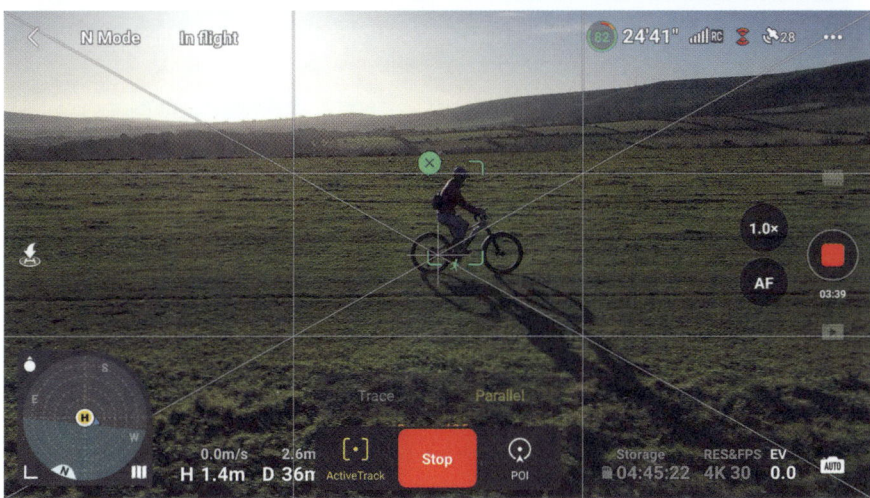

▲ *A screengrab of Active Track in action in the DJI Fly app. It can be hard to focus on riding your bike and paying attention to the drone, so it's usually best to track a friend.*

ASSIGNMENT

33

TIPS

- If you have the option to use a tighter focal length or slight digital zoom, you can make an orbiting shot even more dramatic.

- Use manual exposure to avoid unwanted exposure changes as the lighting changes during the flight.

- Be aware that obstacle avoidance might not be effective for sideways flight (see Assignment 32).

INTO ORBIT

Flying a drone in a circle either clockwise or counterclockwise around a fixed point is a compelling way to draw attention to both your subject matter and the surroundings. It's a dramatic effect that can lend an epic feel to your video, particularly if the subject is in an elevated position or stands out from the background in some way. Your assignment is to produce a short video clip that utilizes this technique.

An "orbit" shot can be achieved in several ways, from fully automated to fully manual flight. Pick a subject that is higher than most of the surrounding landscape. This could be the peak of a hill or mountain, with or without a human subject standing on it, a lone tree, a boat, or a building. To perform the move manually, press record, then push the sticks on your controller gently in opposite directions (left stick left and right stick right or vice versa). This will move the drone to one side while yawing it in the opposite direction. Keep your subject centered in the frame by controlling the relative movement of each stick—this takes some practice but isn't too hard.

For a more automated technique, depending on your drone model, you can use Circle in QuickShots, Point of Interest, or Spotlight mode. They all work in slightly different ways but are easy to grasp. If you are using an automated mode, you will want good light and contrast for the drone to lock onto your subject.

▶ *This fishing boat made a good subject for an orbit, with plenty of space on all sides, helping to give a sense of isolation.*

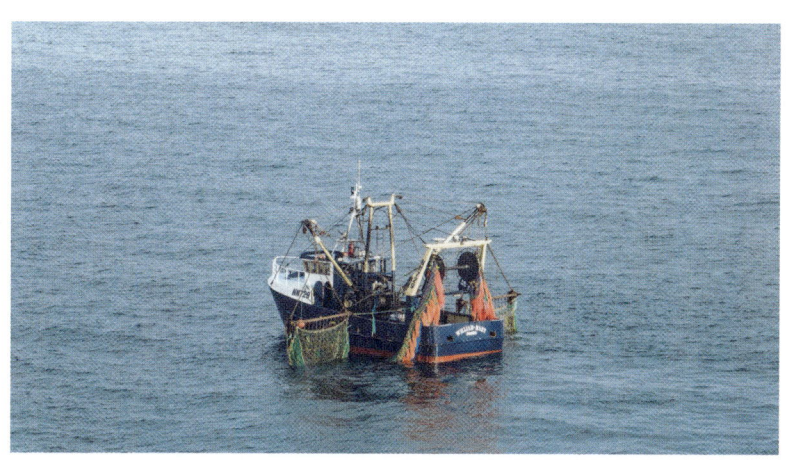

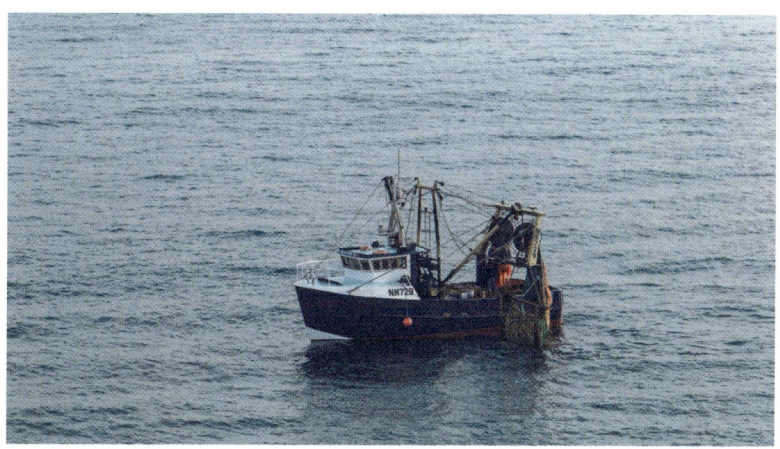

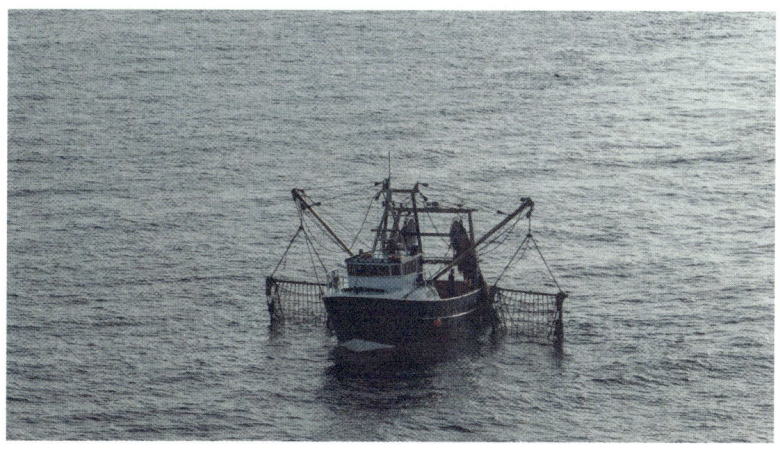

ASSIGNMENT
34

TIPS

- Disable the Return to Home feature and set the drone to hover if signal is lost, otherwise you may find the drone colliding with walls if it has picked up any GPS signal and tries to return to the takeoff point.

- Consider using propeller guards if flying in a tight space to minimize any damage from minor collisions.

- Only shoot stills or video if the drone is flying predictably. A drone that is not 100 percent under your control and a pilot concentrating on the screen is a recipe for collisions.

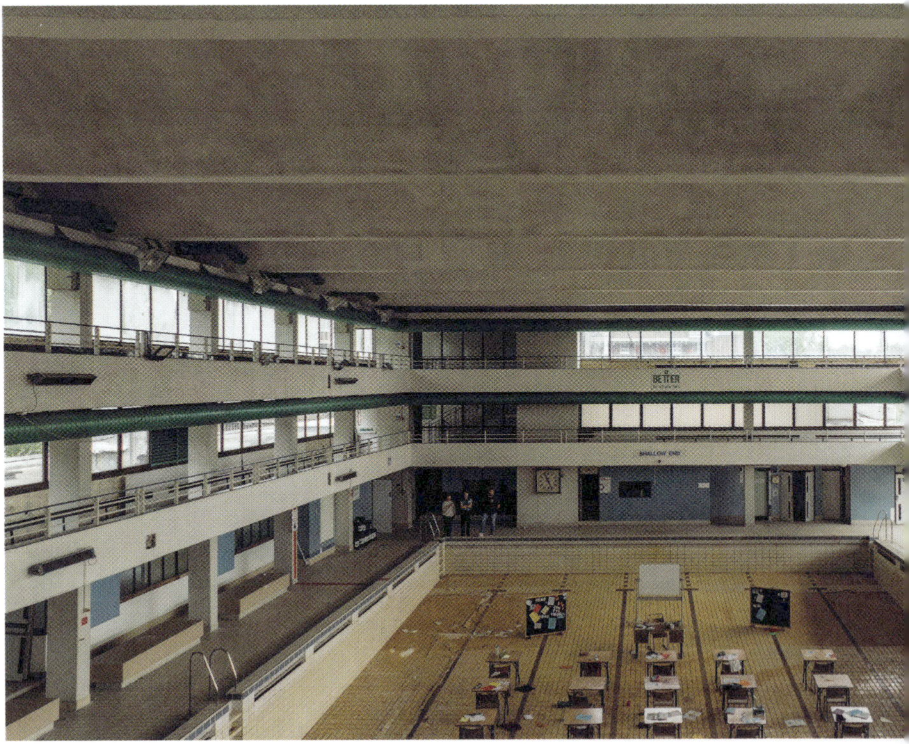

INTERIORS

Interior drone photography is a great skill to work on if you have unsuitable weather outside, be it rain or too much wind, especially if you have access to a large interior space, as a drone can be a fantastic way to achieve otherwise difficult shots. If there is little light available, you will have to use a slow shutter speed or high ISO or both. Fortunately, there shouldn't be any wind adding unwanted motion blur.

For this assignment, you will be using your drone to take stills or video clips inside a building. Be aware that you're unlikely to get a GPS signal indoors, which drones use to stabilize any drift. Most modern drones also have downward-facing vision sensors, which use an image of the floor to stabilize flight. However, these sensors can be fooled, particularly in low light or by shiny surfaces or those with repeating patterns, so be prepared for unpredictable flight behavior.

If you don't have access to a large building, you may still be able to practice interior flying in your own home. If space is tight, disable obstacle avoidance.

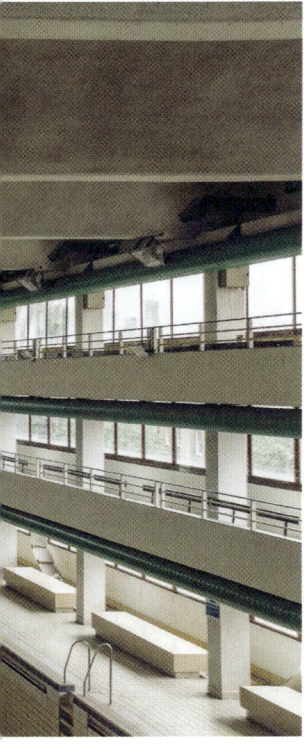

◀ *A large interior space plays to the strengths of drones as a photographic tool. I could get a great perspective by flying the drone close to the ceiling in this abandoned swimming pool.*

ASSIGNMENT JOURNAL

_____

_____

_____

_____

_____

_____

_____

_____

ASSIGNMENT
35

TIPS

- Use manual settings to ensure exposures are consistent across your series of images.

- To simplify post-processing, try to ensure there aren't any moving elements in the areas that will overlap.

DRONECEPTION

The title of this assignment is a reference to the movie *Inception* (2010), in which cities and landscapes are warped into impossible shapes. For this assignment, you will create a still image in this style from a series of drone photographs. Although the drone technique is relatively straightforward, this assignment does require some familiarity with photo editing, including layers and various warping tools.

The most effective results often come from subjects with strong linear features leading into the image. You also want a subject where there is a clear distinction in the horizontal to vertical view, as the background to the image is a top-down view,

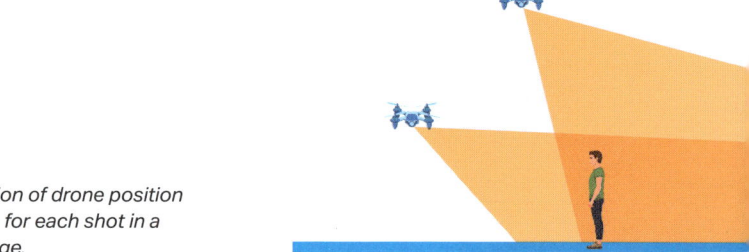

▶ *An approximation of drone position and camera angle for each shot in a droneception image.*

whereas the foreground is at an oblique angle, giving the impression that the ground is bending. Subjects that I have found work well are a road or track, possibly leading to a body of water, as the road provides a continual line into the image, and the water being on a vertical plane in the background adds to the mind-bending illusion.

Take a series of up to six still images, starting a few feet off the ground and progressively flying forward and upward after each shot while tilting the camera further downward. The images should overlap by 25–40 percent. Stop when the drone is considerably higher and further forward than the starting point, with the camera angled vertically down (see diagram below). It takes some practice to get your positions optimized for your scene, so be prepared for some trial and error.

Back at your computer, assign each photo to a separate layer on a long, thin canvas, with the first (lowest) photo at the bottom of the frame and the last (highest, top-down) photo at the top of the frame. Distort and warp each photo so that the features line up with the same features on the adjacent photos. Again, this will take some trial and error, but the effort is worth it.

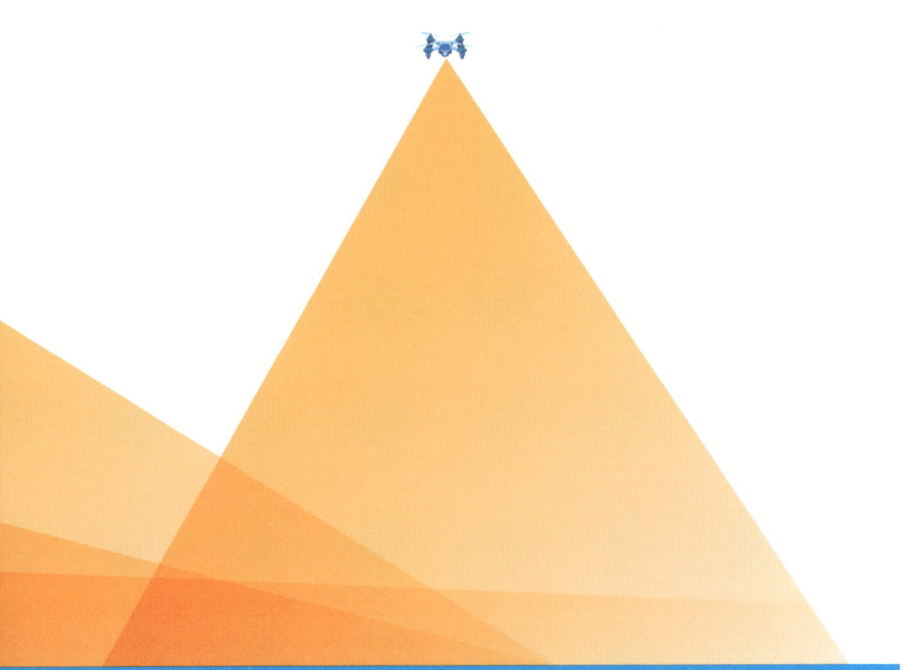

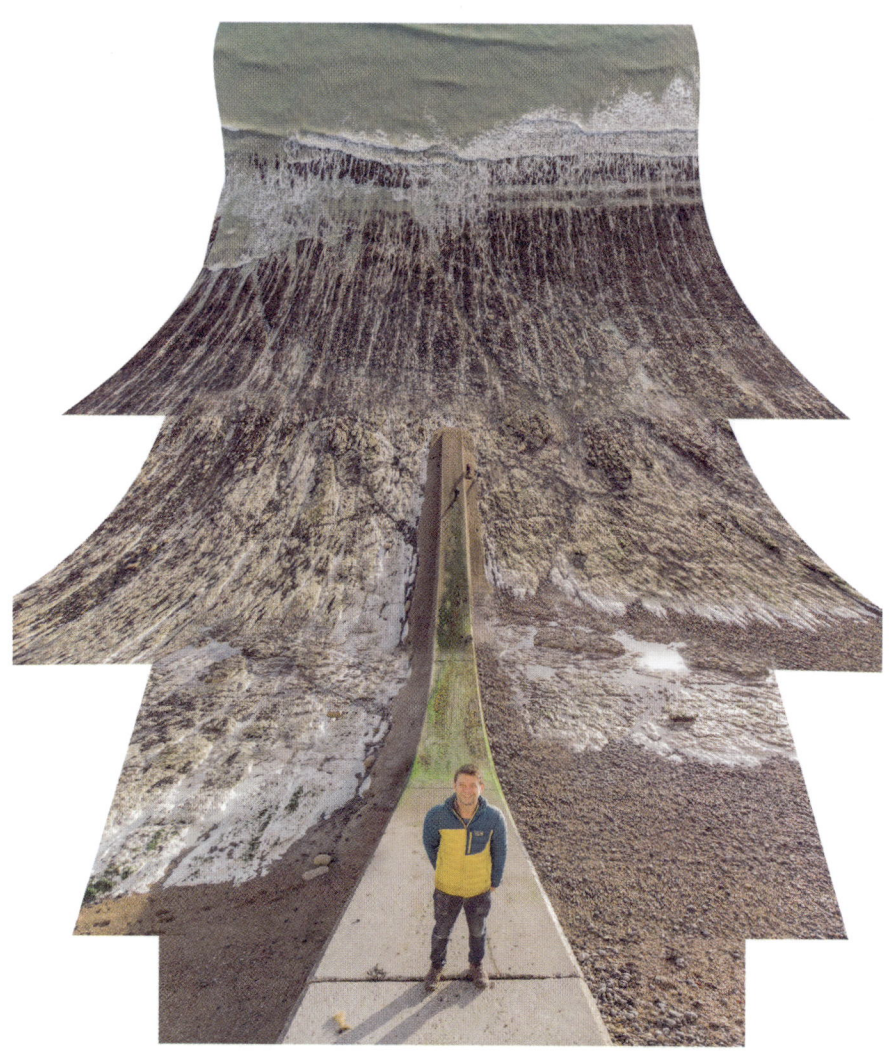

▲ The image before being cropped,
showing how the layers have been warped.

▶ The finished result is a mind-bending
optical illusion—the breakwater adds a
good linear reference point.

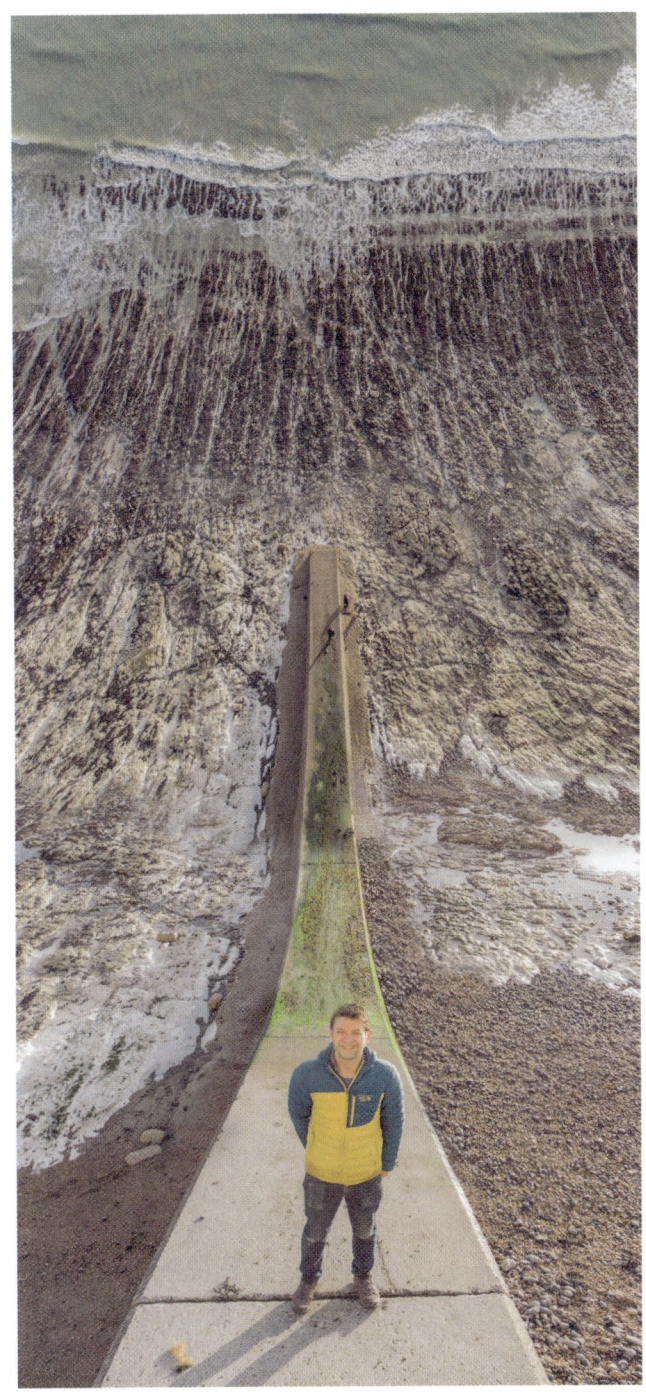

- Look at the drone not your screen, particularly when the drone is close to you, as it's much better if your face is in the video rather than the top of your head.

- Choose an environment with some interest rather than an open, uniform field. Beside a river or lake, on top of a hill, or outside a house or building could all work well.

- A sunny day will give better results than overcast conditions, as the bright and saturated colors and extra contrast add to the mini-world effect.

ASTEROID VIDEO

Asteroid is a QuickShot mode available in many models of drone. The result is a video that starts on the drone pilot, flies away before the scene warps into a "little planet" (stereographic projection of a 360° image), before flying back into the pilot. It's a novel effect and great for posting on social media.

For your assignment, pick a spot without any obstacles, being aware that the drone is going to fly backward and upward from a starting point facing you at low altitude. You will need a full battery, as the final part of the capture process takes some time.

The flight is fully automated, so always keep an eye on the drone and be prepared to cancel the flight if any hazards arise. After a brief pause while the video is compiled by the app, you should be able to review the results on screen. This will give you a feel for the output and allow you to make changes and try again if necessary.

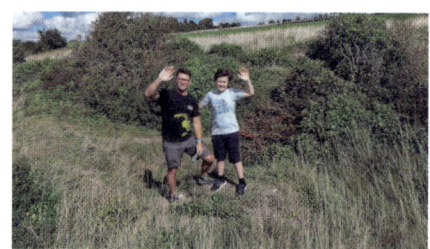

▼ *Screengrabs from an Asteroid video clip
—software automatically blends video with
a 360° still image.*

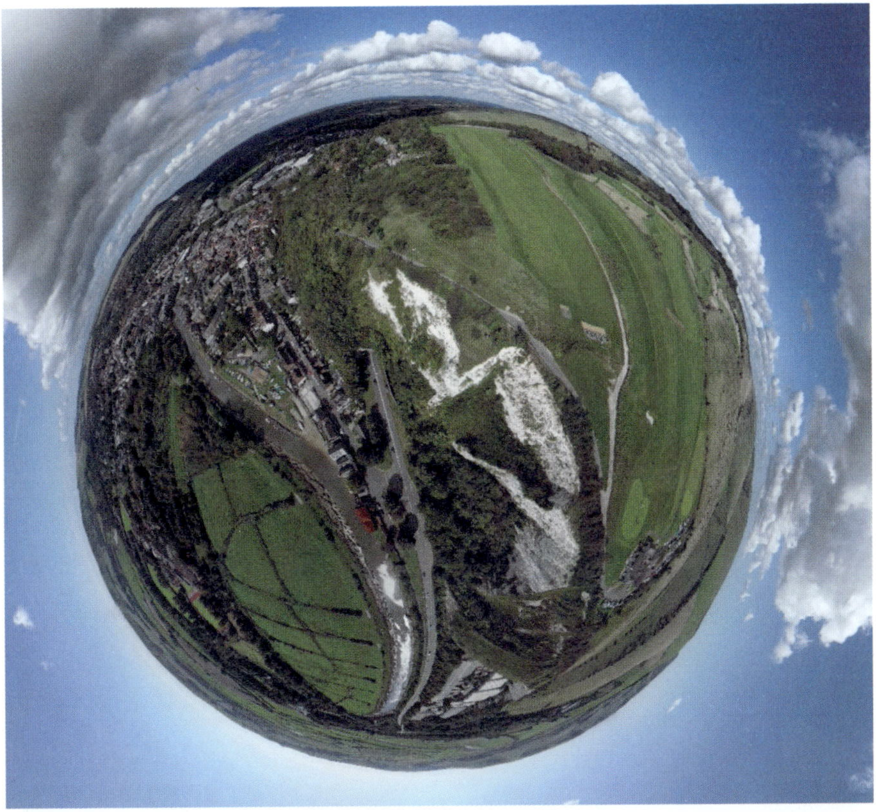

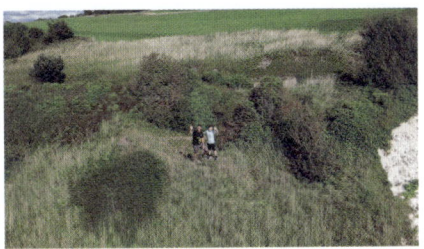

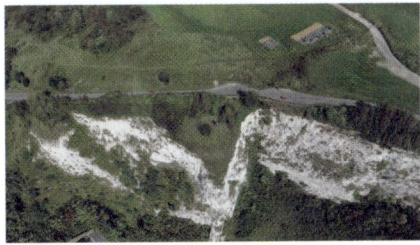

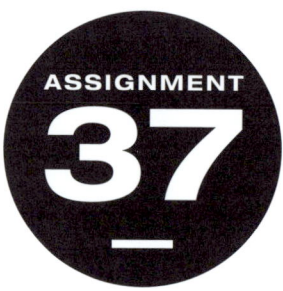

ASSIGNMENT
37

TIPS

- Make sure your drone has adequate LED lighting for you to maintain a clear visual line of sight.

- Choose an evening with little or no wind to avoid unwanted camera shake.

- Shooting in Raw format will give you more flexibility when post-processing, as no data is lost to image compression.

▼ *I had arranged permission from London City Airport and informed the police of the flight before I took this photo of Canary Wharf and the O2 Arena. This is a panorama of three images stitched together.*

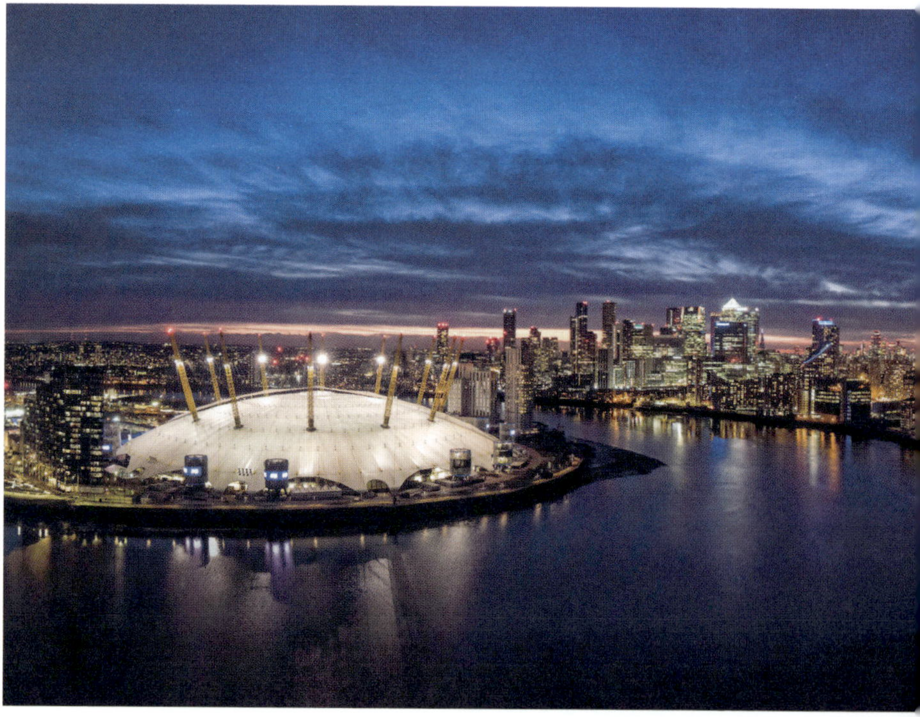

BRIGHT LIGHTS, BIG CITY

As daylight fades and streetlights and buildings start to shine, cities take on a whole new look, with the gray concrete expanse replaced with rows of brightly lit windows, neon signs, and bustling bars and restaurants. Your assignment is to take a drone photograph of a town or city after the sun has gone down, taking advantage of the artificial lights and nocturnal glow.

After ensuring that your flight is legal and you have satisfied any airspace requirements or permissions, select a takeoff point where you have adequate clearance from public and buildings and where you have a direct line of sight to your drone's vantage point. Remember that buildings and Wi-Fi interference could block your signal. Also, your drone's obstacle avoidance may not work well in low light. If you need to tap to focus, you'll need an area with good contrast.

It's best to use manual exposure settings to maintain good control over ISO and shutter speed. Avoid very high ISO settings—on small drones, ISO 800 might be the maximum for good image quality. This will likely mean a shutter speed of up to a second or two, so make sure the drone isn't moving during the exposure by not touching any of the flight controls. Taking several identical shots will give you the best chance of getting a sharp one with no motion blur. You may get the nicest shots before the sky is fully dark—a little bit of color and texture in the sky adds interest.

POST-PROCESSING

Play around with the white balance settings to achieve the best look. If it's not fully dark, you will be dealing with a mixture of cold (blue) natural light and warm (orange) artificial light. Finding a good color balance is key to a successful shot, as you want colors to look as accurate and realistic as possible.

ASSIGNMENT
38

▼ *This three-shot stitched panorama of Wadi Rum in Jordan was taken using a DJI Phantom 4. When flying in the desert, sand gets everywhere, so a takeoff and landing pad is a good idea.*

TIPS

• Avoid large expanses of water, as the featureless surface makes automated stitching difficult.

• Use manual exposure and white balance, as any automatic changes in settings may be visible in the final panorama.

POST-PROCESSING

Most editing software has a panorama stitching feature that will automatically align and merge multiple images to produce a panoramic shot. After you have output your panorama, you can apply your usual adjustments, including slight crops, if needed.

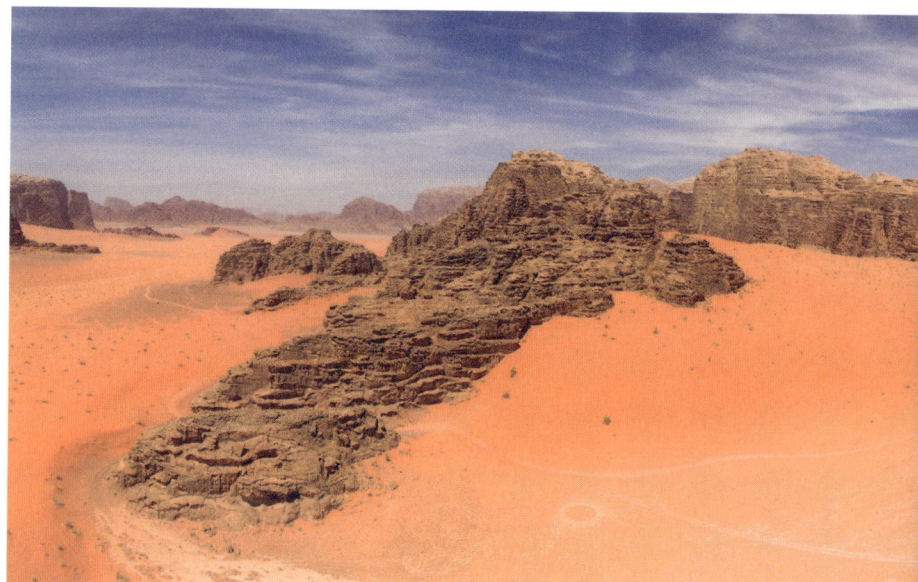

GET PANORAMIC

Some vistas are just too big to fit in one shot. This is where a stitched panorama comes to the rescue. It's a super-handy technique to have in your repertoire, particularly when backing away further isn't possible due to the need to maintain a visual line of sight to your drone. In this assignment, your mission is to create a stitched panorama of a super-wide landscape that includes interesting details, colors, and a dramatic sense of vastness.

The technique is relatively simple. Some drones have an automated panorama feature that will stitch multiple photos together in camera to produce a high-resolution 180º shot. But even if your drone doesn't support this feature, it's not difficult to achieve great results manually. First, yaw the drone from left to right to establish the start and end point of your panorama, then check that your exposure settings work across the whole of the panorama. If the sun blows out the sky in part of the panorama, underexpose a little and bring up the dark areas in post-processing.

Yaw your drone to the first frame (I usually work left to right) and take the shot, then yaw until you have 30 to 50-percent overlap with the previous frame. It helps to take note of a reference point on the right of the frame and then yaw until it's 30 to 50 percent from the left edge of your new frame. Take another shot and repeat until you've reached the end point of your panorama.

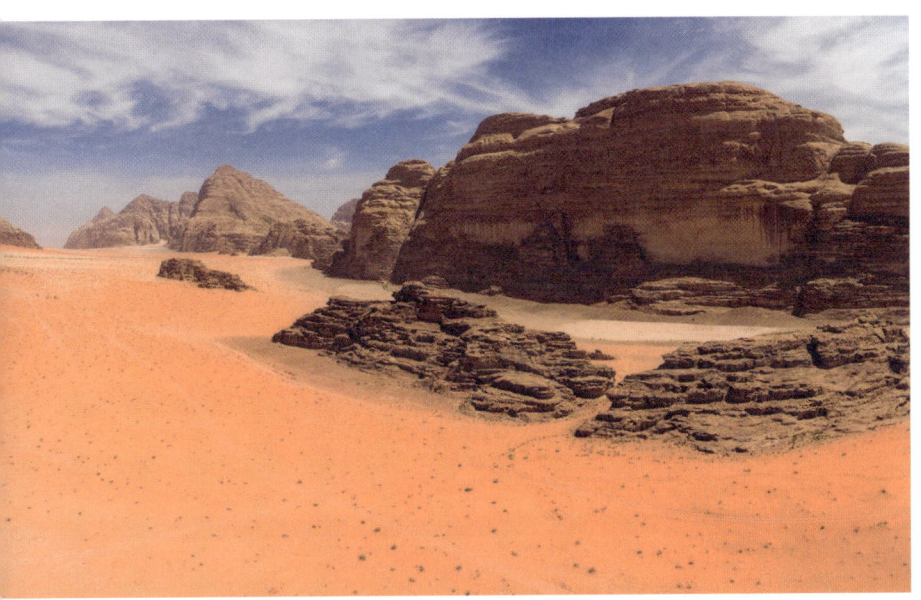

TIPS

- Roads heading into the frame can make useful leading lines, directing the eye to a central subject such as a busy junction.

- In terms of composition, make a deliberate decision about the orientation of the road or roads, and make small movements to the drone until the arrangement looks most pleasing. Find the most eye-catching shapes and place them at strategic points in the frame.

THE ROAD LESS TRAVELED

We spend a lot of time traveling along roads but may not be aware of their potential as subject matter for drone imagery. They are often of contrasting color or tone to their background, which makes them stand out nicely, and road markings can add extra interest. For this assignment, your brief is to take a creative drone photograph of a road or junction, using strong shapes and leading lines to add visual interest.

Always be aware of the rules surrounding drones and roads. Even if it's legal to fly closer, keep a healthy distance from roads to avoid distracting drivers. When planning a composition, avoid heavily congested areas, both in terms of road users and pedestrians. Dusk or nighttime can look great if there is some street lighting, and you may be able to capture the trails of vehicle lights if you use a long exposure. Just remember that wind will affect the stability of the drone and potentially cause motion blur so look for still weather. In calm conditions, you should be able to get some sharp shots even at 1 sec. or longer.

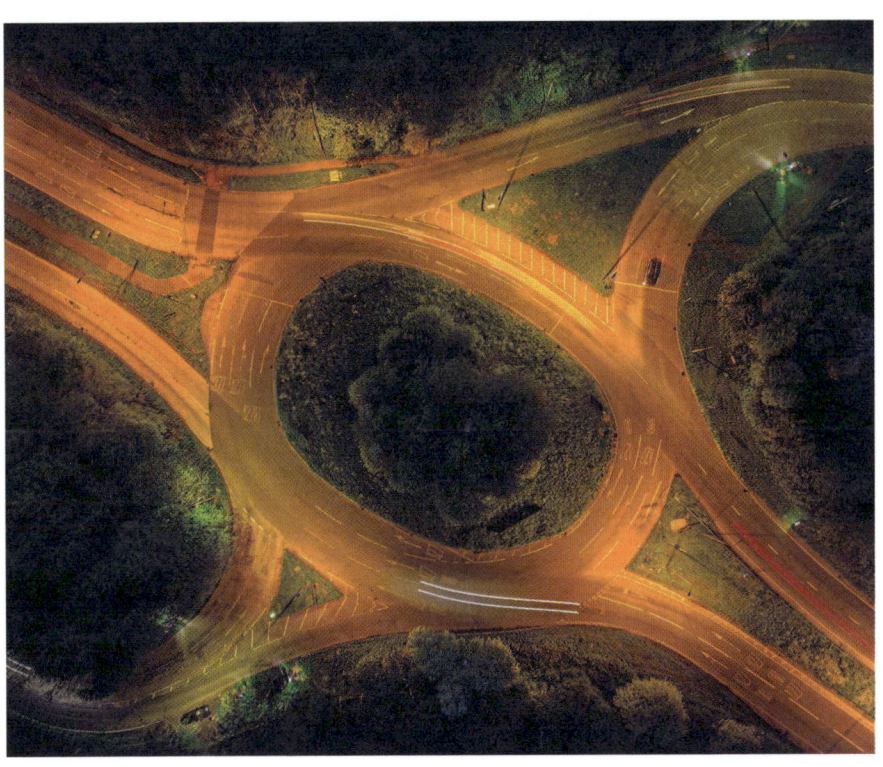

ASSIGNMENT JOURNAL

▲ *This roundabout was photographed late in the blue hour with a 1-sec. exposure to produce light trails from the cars. The tungsten bulbs in the streetlights give an orange hue to the road, which could be corrected by adjusting the white balance, but I like this color palette.*

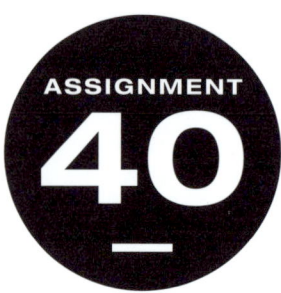

ASSIGNMENT

40

TIPS

- You may find a perpendicular view from over the middle of the river works best, perhaps with some reflections in the water. An oblique angle with perspective lines leading into the background might also work well.

- If it's a very large bridge, you may need to maintain a significant distance to fit the whole structure in the frame, so plan your takeoff and landing point accordingly.

▼ *The scale of the Forth Bridges in Scotland was too large to be able to safely operate the drone over the middle of the channel, so I elevated the drone above my position on the estuary bank.*

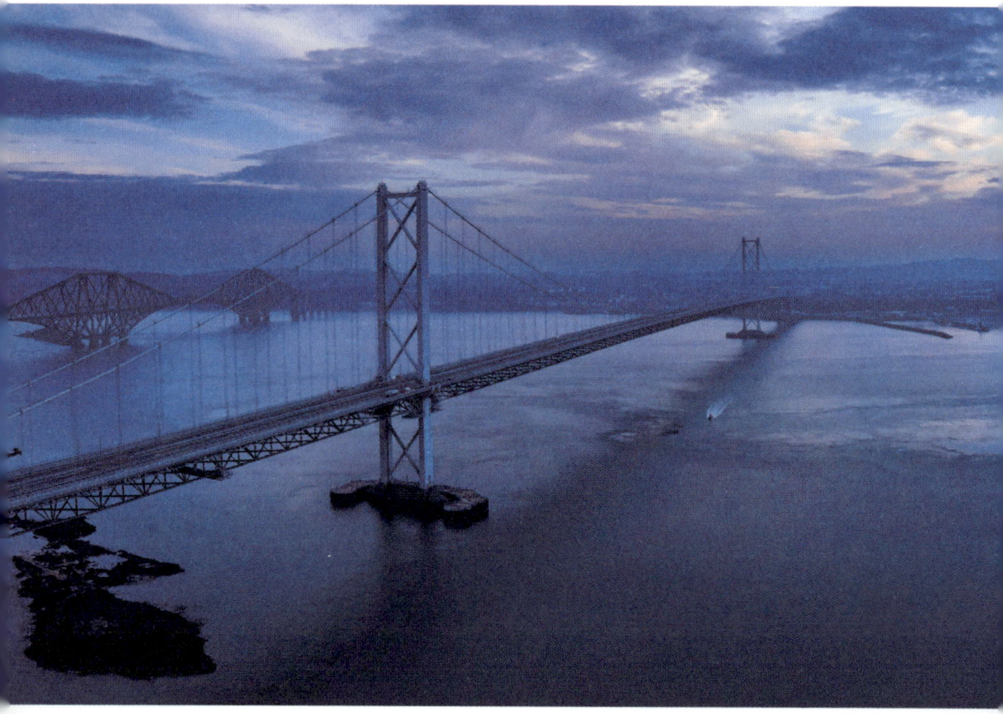

BRIDGING THE GAP

Being able to operate easily over water makes drones a great tool for bridge photography. Apart from the bridge itself, there are generally few obstacles to worry about, and as subject matter bridges can offer a variety of possibilities from square-on side elevations to vertigo-inducing top-down perspectives and everything in between. Your task is to take a striking drone photograph of a bridge, using height, perspective, and lighting to show the structure at its best. Consider the angle of the sun—do you want the bridge backlit or frontlit? Perhaps you could frame a sunrise or sunset under the bridge?

Depending on the surroundings of your bridge, there are a few hazards to be aware of. If you plan on flying under any foliage, be aware that you may lose GPS lock and the drone may use downward-facing optical sensors to stabilize itself. If it's over water, these sensors won't work well due to its ever-changing reflectance, resulting in erratic and unstable flight. It's also inadvisable to fly under a bridge, not only because of GPS interference, but also because if you lose control frequency, the drone may ascend to RTH altitude and collide with the underside of the bridge.

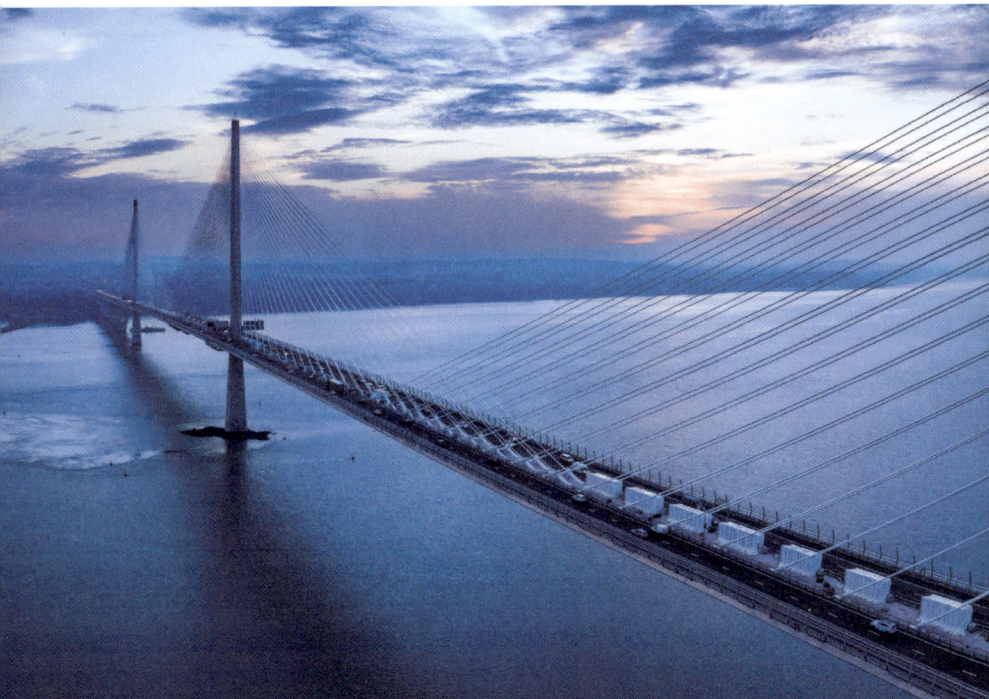

TIPS

- Piloted aircraft often transit lower over the ocean or waterways, so be careful when flying your drone near water. Generally, piloted aircraft must stay 400ft (120m) above populated areas, but they can fly lower over open country or the sea, putting them in potential conflict with drones.

- If you want to make the most of oceanfront lights, the best time of day is often dusk, as this is when artificial lights will show up nicely and there's still just enough ambient light to illuminate at least some detail in the shadow areas.

- Windless evenings are best for low-light shots, as this will minimize unwanted camera shake.

THE WATERFRONT

Where flying a drone over towns and cities can be problematic due to regulations and obstacles, open water gives you plenty of space in which to fly around freely. This assignment is all about taking advantage of this open space and capturing a drone photograph of an urban area meeting the water. Oceanfronts always make for interesting drone images, but lakes and rivers can be just as fascinating.

Think about the type of shot you want to take and the elements you could include. Will it be a top-down shot or a low-angled shot? If shooting at night, could you include the reflections of city lights? Are there any familiar landmarks that could be featured in the photograph? What about roads or promenades? Perhaps you could use these as leading lines or horizontal compositional elements?

▶ *Bright oceanside illuminations create an interesting abstract composition of a pier— I had to be at maximum flight altitude to fit it in the frame.*

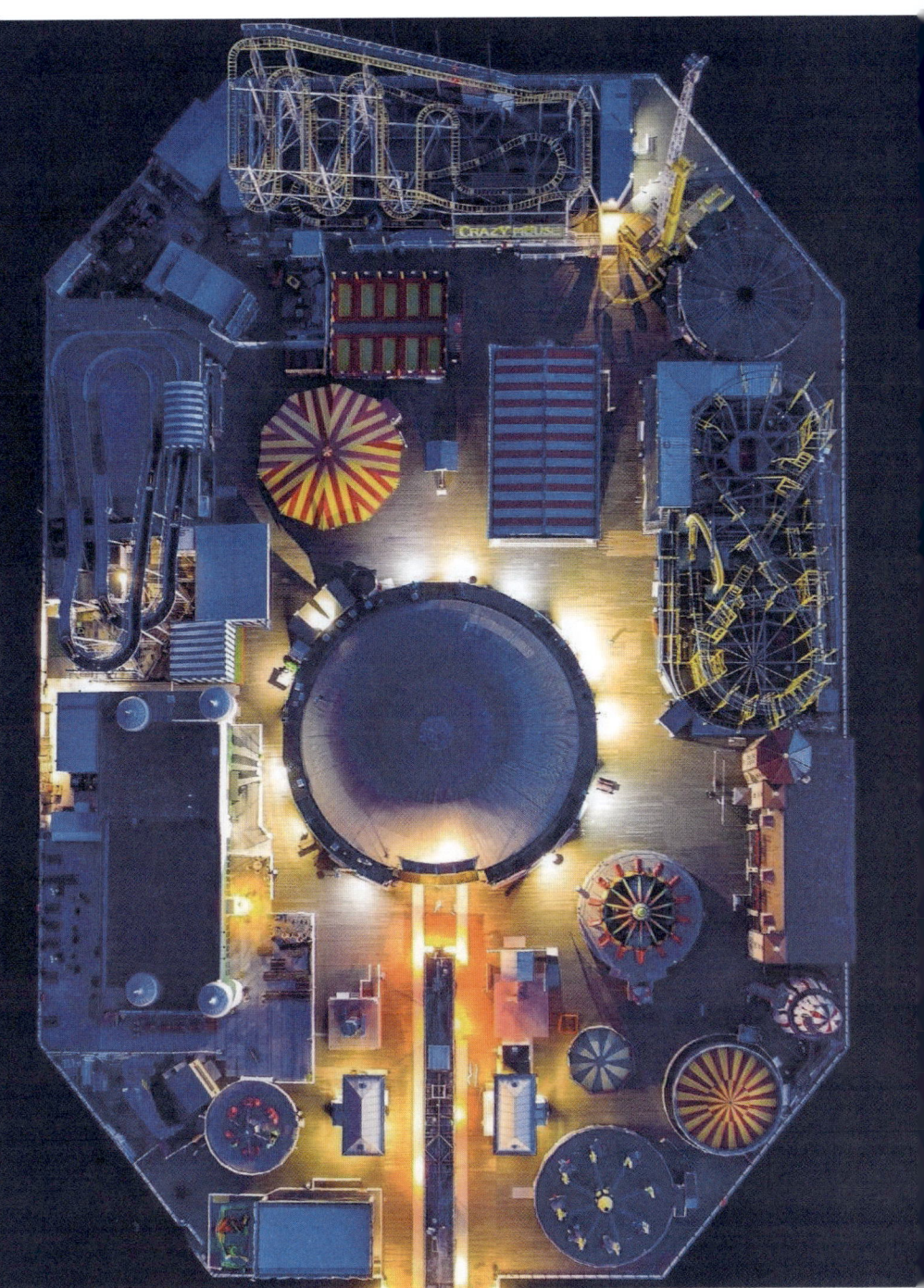

ASSIGNMENT

42

TIPS

- Lone trees are the sort of subject matter that may be best spotted by chance from the road, so keep your eyes peeled for suitable subjects during your car journeys.

- Consider repeating shots of the same tree from the same angle in different seasons for a striking series of shots.

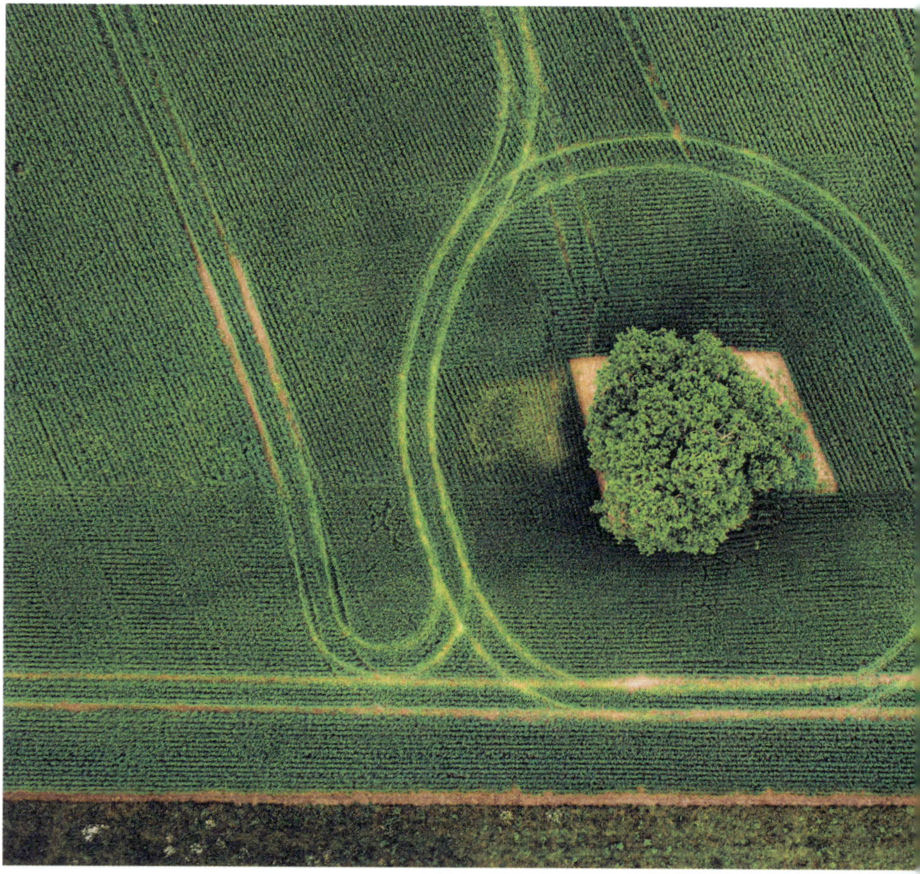

LONE TREE

A lone tree can make the perfect subject for a beautiful, minimalist composition. Different types of trees have very different shapes, and many will change their appearance significantly with the seasons. Your assignment is to shoot a lone tree in the landscape, either from directly above for a top-down perspective or from a more oblique angle. If it's a sunny day, the tree's shadow could form an integral part of the image.

Think about the texture of the ground surrounding the tree. Features may be exaggerated by taking the shot with a low-angled sun. The branches of a dead or leafless tree might cast an intricate shadow. As ever, be mindful of wildlife, particularly as trees often host bird nests, so avoid flying close to them wherever possible in order to avoid disturbing them or causing distress.

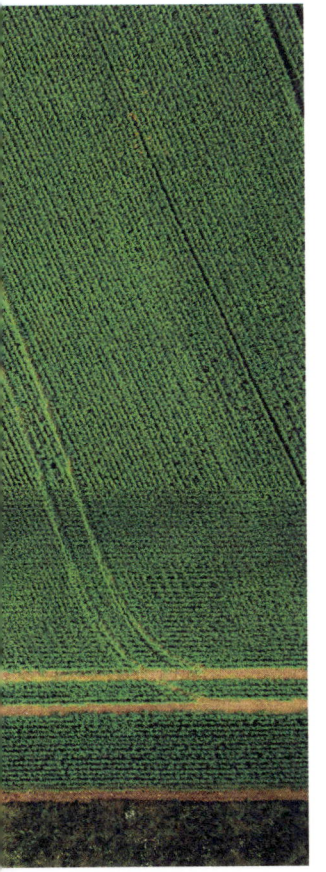

Provided you are in an open area with few obstructions, a lone tree may be an ideal opportunity to shoot from different angles relative to the direction of the light. Try backlighting, front lighting, and side lighting and see how it affects the textures and hues of the leaves.

ASSIGNMENT JOURNAL

◄ *I decided on a top-down view of this oak tree in a wheat field, emphasizing the tramlines made by farm vehicles.*

ASSIGNMENT

43

TIPS

- Use satellite imagery to discover hidden locations and subjects and identify safe takeoff and landing spots.

- If possible, do some prior research on the wreck or building. This could inform your drone photography or simply add an interesting caption.

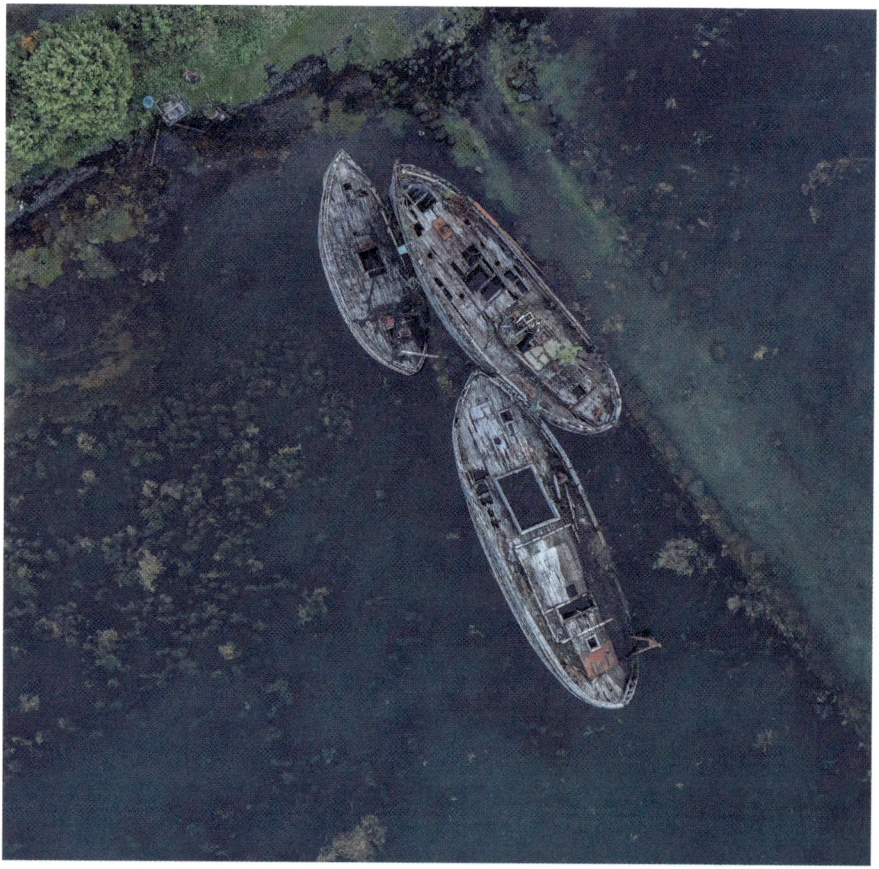

WRECKS AND RUINS

Exploring abandoned buildings and ship graveyards can be a fascinating experience and a drone's eye view can often reveal previously unseen shapes and details. Wrecks and ruins can also tell stories. For instance, trees or vegetation growing through old buildings tell of the passage of time.

Your mission is to find an interesting ruin and shoot a drone image of it in its natural environment, either from directly above or from eye level—a drone may also allow you to access areas that are too dangerous or inaccessible to explore on foot, so you may not even need to take it particularly high.

While these types of areas can appear deserted, always make sure you're not trespassing on private property and don't take risks around unsafe structures. A drone can offer a relatively safe way to explore abandoned areas.

POST-PROCESSING

A subtle HDR look and desaturated colors can add to the atmosphere of shots of abandoned areas. This can be achieved by boosting the exposure of the shadow areas and reducing the highlights, while perhaps also reducing saturation a touch.

ASSIGNMENT JOURNAL

◄ *Shipwrecks on the banks of a loch in Scotland. The muted colors add to the sense of melancholy and abandonment.*

ASSIGNMENT
44

TIPS

- Make sure your drone has updated its home point before taking off to fly over water. If you don't, you risk it hovering over the water until the battery dies if you lose your signal.

- Avoid midday sun to reduce sunglint off the water or you may find you have a distracting bright spot in your image.

AHOY THERE!

Even familiar subjects can look like abstract shapes when viewed from above, and boats are no exception—it may take viewers a few moments to figure out what they're looking at. Boats are also usually positioned against neutral backgrounds, which makes them stand out, particularly if their decks are brightly colored.

Your assignment is to take a drone image of a boat that takes advantage of strong contrasts and/or interesting shapes. For instance, if you've found a port or marina, try to arrange the pontoons or jetties into a pleasing composition, perhaps running vertically, horizontally, or diagonally. Try a few options by yawing and shifting the drone.

If the boats are white, there's a danger of blown highlights, so you might want to underexpose by a stop or two. Also consider boats that are underway, as the wake from the boat often adds an interesting compositional element. Just be careful you don't let the drone get too far away so that you can't see it.

POST-PROCESSING

In many locations, the water color may be muddy and unattractive. If you shoot Raw images, you can maximize your options for adjusting the color balance of the water, perhaps shifting it toward blue or green.

▶ The neat lines of the pontoon and yachts make for an interesting abstract composition.

▶ This large ship could only fit in the frame from an altitude of 400ft (120m), with the addition of a wideangle lens accessory.

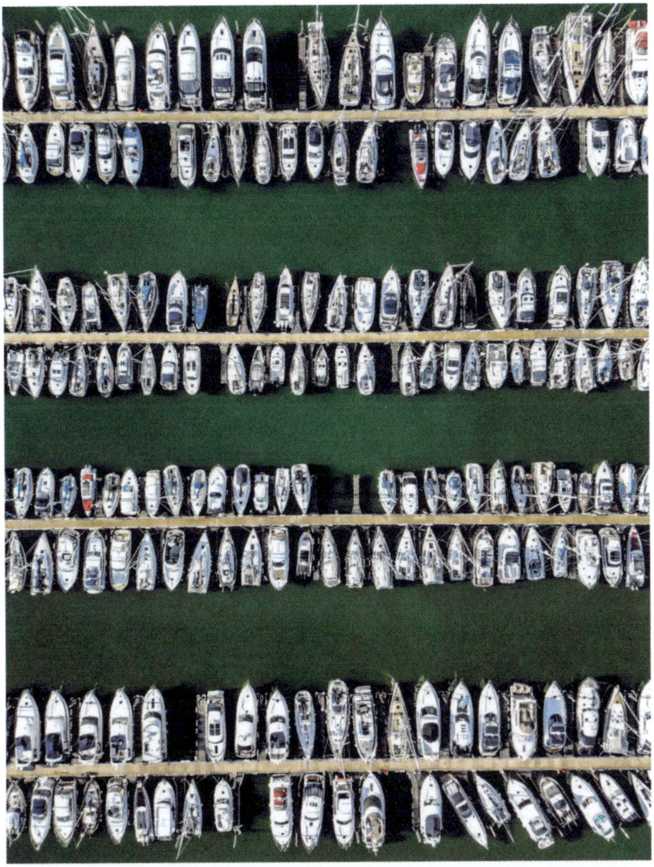

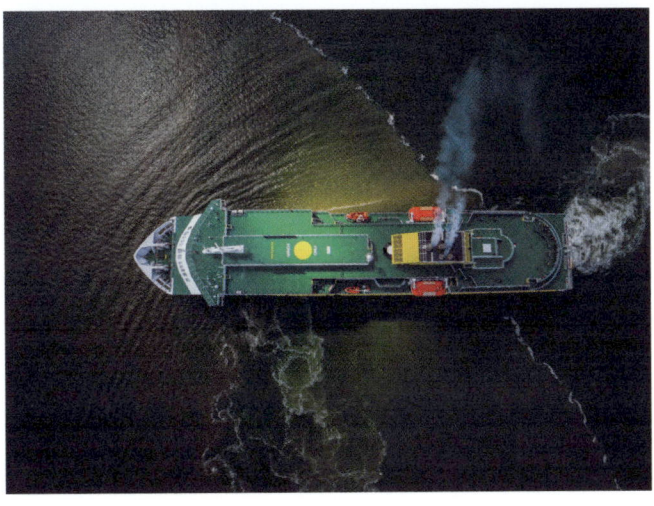

ASSIGNMENT
45
—

TIPS

• Save your screenshots from previous visits to a separate device or print them out for reference, so you can line up features to precisely reproduce the shot.

• Use an app to predict the position of the sun in your shot at different times of day or different dates. PhotoPillls or The Photographer's Ephemeris are ideal.

• Shooting in full sun will emphasize changes in direction of lighting and shadows.

▶ *Three images of a windmill taken at different times on the same day show the changes in lighting. Left to right: 8am, 3pm, 7.30pm.*

ASSIGNMENT JOURNAL

_____

_____

_____

_____

_____

_____

_____

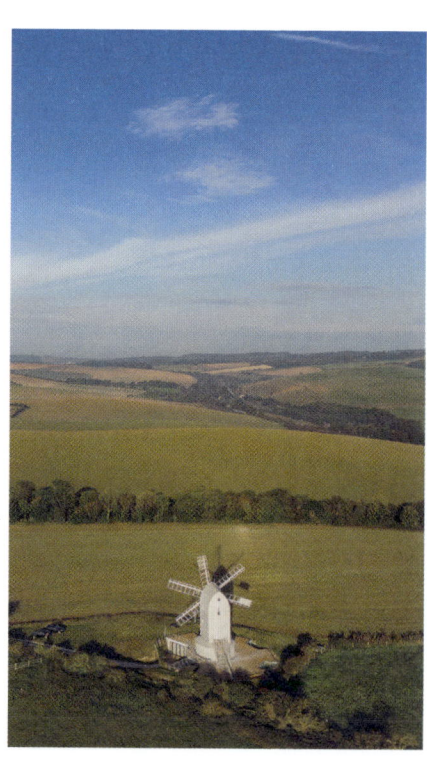

TIME SLICE

Time slices are composite images taken from the same location and composed of vertical strips taken at different moments, capturing the progression of time in a single frame. For this assignment, you will produce a time slice of a favorite location, highlighting differences in weather, seasons, and lighting.

Many drones feature waypoint missions, which record the exact location, drone orientation, and camera angle so they can be repeated exactly later. Depending on your model, this feature may only be available in Hyperlapse mode, but you can still use it to take still shots. Even if you don't have waypoint missions as a feature, you can still complete this assignment—just remember your exact takeoff point and fly vertically up for your picture, then record the exact height, compose and take your photo, and screenshot it for future reference. You should be able to align features exactly on future visits.

In post-processing, make identically sized vertical crops of your time-slice images and position them side by side on a blank canvas. You may need to make minor adjustments to the crop to optimize alignment.

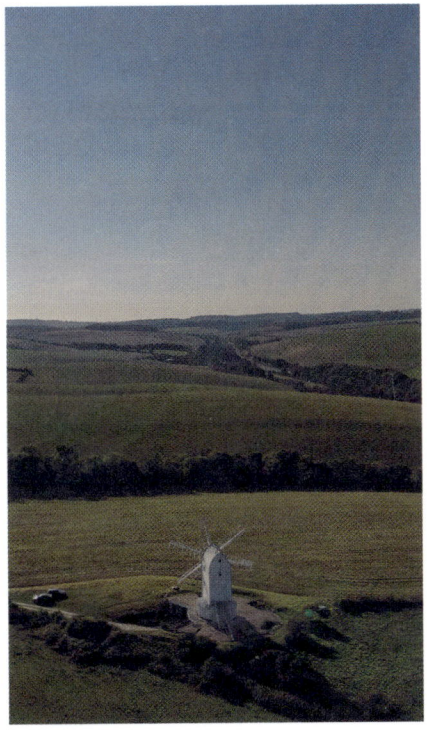 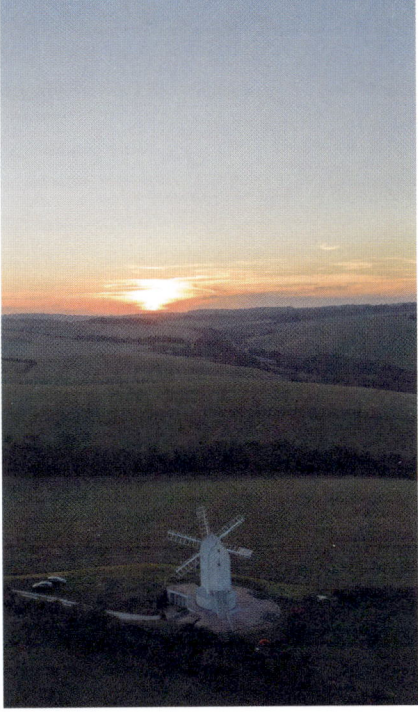

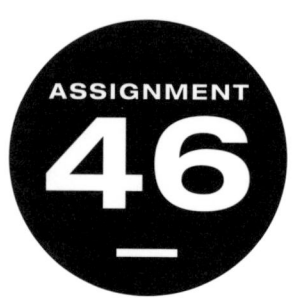

ASSIGNMENT

46

TIPS

- Experiment with neutral density (ND) filters if you have any, as the addition of a filter or accessory lens may alter the characteristics of the lens flare.

- If you can't quite get the flare in the right part of the frame, trying again at a different time of day might fix the issue, as the sun's angle keeps on changing.

LENS FLARE

Lens flare is an effect that many photographers try to avoid, but it can also be a fun and atmospheric creative effect, adding a "summery" vibe or instilling a retro look. The style and characteristics of the flare will vary according to the lens on your drone and whether you have any filters fitted. Generally, you see flare when the lens is pointed toward the light source (usually the sun).

For this assignment, your task is to shoot a drone landscape that incorporates attractive lens flare. You can fine-tune the effect by tilting the camera or yawing the drone a small amount. You may then need to adjust the position of the drone to get the composition you want—a wideangle lens accessory will give you more options.

With my drone, I found I could get a nice "light leak" effect with the sun just out of frame close to sunset—this is the look that you got with old film cameras when extraneous light leaked onto the film plane, creating orange-hued patches. You may want to adjust your exposure manually to control overexposed parts of the image.

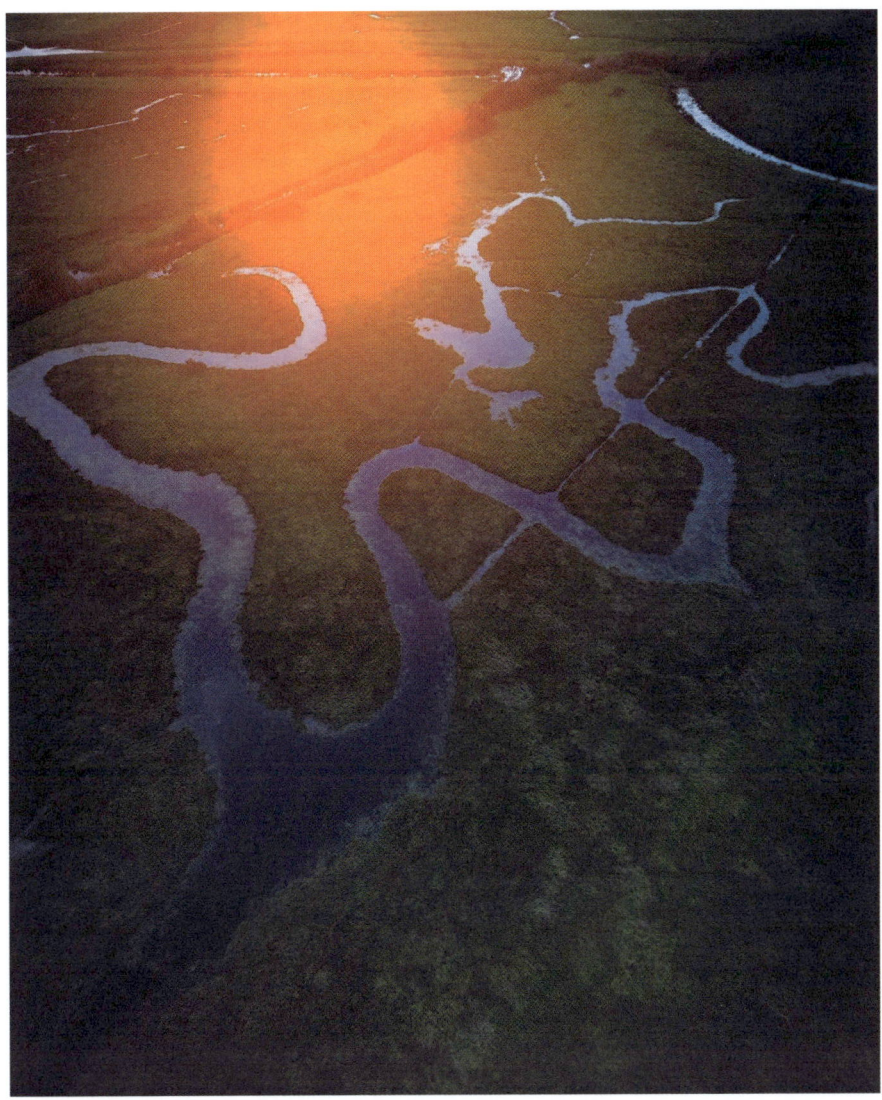

POST-PROCESSING

This type of image often lends itself to a dreamy summer look, so consider warming up the white balance and increasing the saturation.

▲ *The sun just out of frame produces a flare that emulates a retro light leak on this shot of river channels at sunset.*

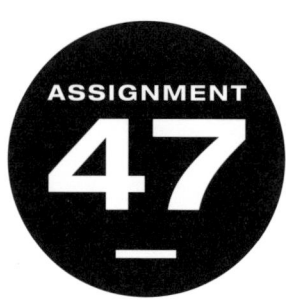

ASSIGNMENT
47

TIPS

- Use satellite imagery to plan your shoot in advance. Some programs allow you to measure the dimensions of your area of interest, so you can estimate the number of rows and columns of images you will need.

- If you can choose an area with some interesting topography, these features will come alive in a 3D-elevation map.

POST-PROCESSING

You can make your 3D map either online in the cloud if you're using a mapping app, or in a photo editor. Check that your editor can support multi-row stitching. If not, you may still be able to stitch columns and rows separately.

ASSIGNMENT JOURNAL

▶ *This image of a saltmarsh is composed of around 20 images and covers an area around 1000ft (300m) wide.*

MAPPING MISSION

It sometimes happens that you find an interesting top-down shot, but the area you want to capture is too large to fit in the frame from 400ft (120m), which is the maximum permitted altitude in many countries. When this is the case, it's possible to fly a grid mission, where you shoot many still photos with the camera pointing straight down and stitch them together afterward. So, for this assignment, your task is to embark on an aerial adventure, shooting multiple top-down images to "map" your epic drone landscape.

Apps such as Drone Deploy and Pix4D will do this as an automated mission, flying the drone and shooting the appropriate number of images to cover a predetermined area. These images are then stitched and processed into a 3D map in the cloud.

If you don't have access to such apps, you can fly the mission manually, taking a grid of overlapping images and making sure you have at least 30-percent overlap between rows and columns of images. If you want to make a 3D map, you'll need at least 70-percent overlap. You'll also need to find an area with unique features that the stitching software can identify as common points in overlapping areas, so avoid featureless areas such as sand and water.

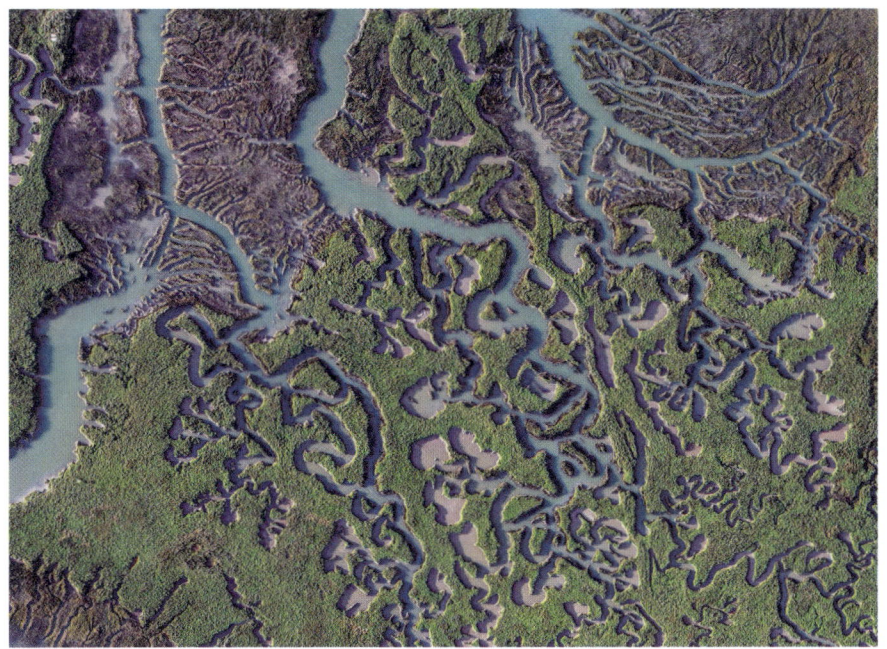

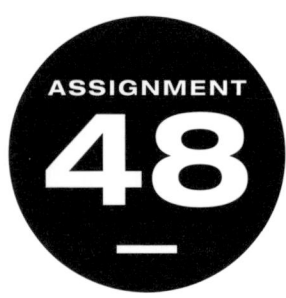

ASSIGNMENT
48

TIPS

- If you are moving under your own power, pack light to save energy. Given the choice, go with a small, light drone.

- If you're packing lots of equipment, keep the drone accessible so you can quickly grab it and launch it when you spot a good shot.

▶ *While exploring Hardangervidda, Norway, on skis, I was able to fly my drone in temperatures down to -13ºF (-25ºC) with some careful planning.*

ASSIGNMENT JOURNAL

_____

_____

_____

_____

_____

_____

_____

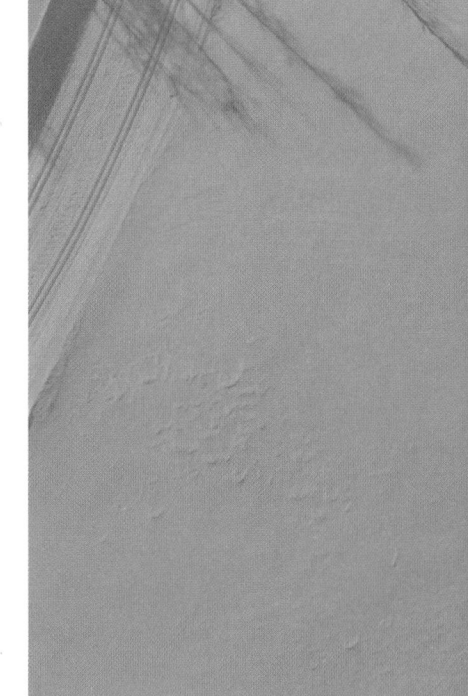

LIFE'S AN ADVENTURE

It's time to head off the beaten track and use your drone to document your adventures in wilderness areas. This could be desert, a frozen wasteland, vast tracts of forested land, a mountain range, or simply your local hills. The point of this assignment is to showcase a remote area.

You may not have access to power for charging batteries, so either bring plenty of charged batteries or a large USB powerpack. If temperatures fall below 50°F (10°C), you'll need to keep the flight batteries warm before the flight or you risk a drone that refuses to take off or suddenly loses power. I often keep batteries warm in the bottom of my sleeping bag overnight, and in an inside pocket during the day.

You might want to emphasize the vast scale of the landscape or the harshness or beauty of the wilderness. Human figures or a tent relatively small in the frame will provide a sense of scale. Remember that if you are in a mountainous area, you can expect turbulent and unpredictable winds, so always be mindful of the weather. Also, many wilderness areas are national parks or nature reserves so always check that you're allowed to fly your drone there.

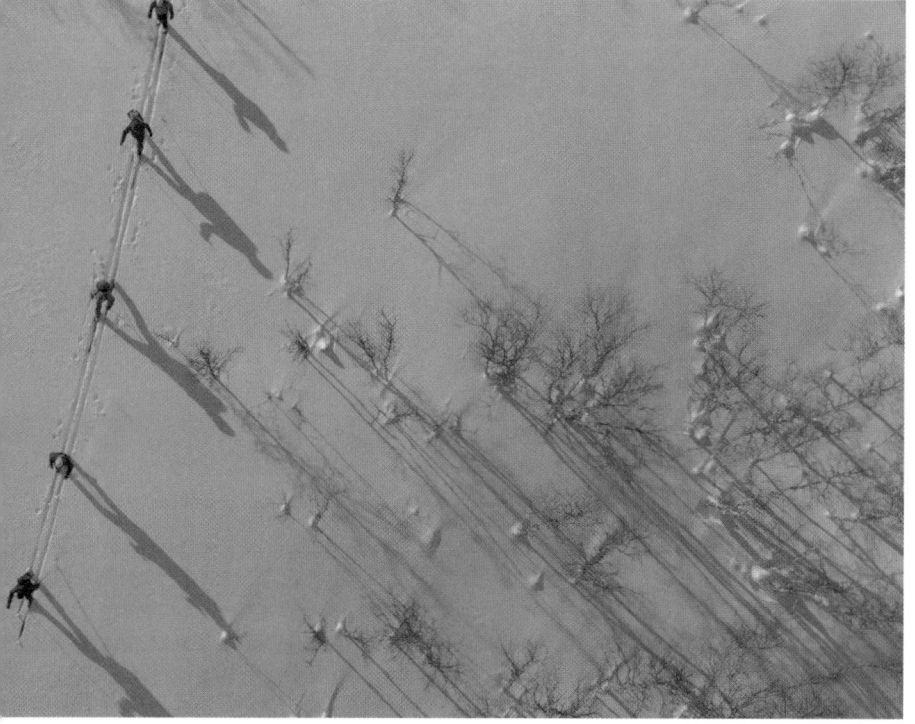

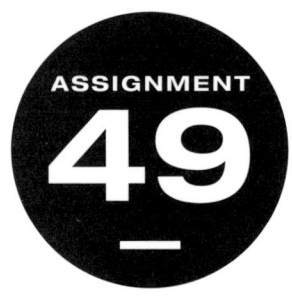

ASSINGMENT
49

TIPS

- Spend time exploring an area from the air to get a feel for the textural appearance of different surfaces.

- Textures can take on a different appearance from different heights so don't be afraid to fly both high and low.

▶ *Different textures can add to an interesting abstract composition, as can be seen in this image of a plowed field meeting grassland.*

▶ *This shot of a jetty at the edge of an estuary highlights different textures of water and sand. It was not the exact shot I set out to achieve but I noticed it once the drone was in the air.*

TOP-DOWN TEXTURES

It's easy to overlook the role of textures in adding to the success of an image, but they can add a subtle and often unexpected element to a composition. For this assignment, you will take a top-down drone photo in which texture plays a large part.

You can find interesting textures in a wide variety of settings. Consider agricultural land, forests, coasts and beaches, bodies of water, and even artificial surfaces. If the texture has any directionality to it, give some thought to how it is aligned with respect to the framing of your shot. If you have several textures in a shot, pay attention to how they are balanced. Lighting plays a big part in how a texture appears, with flat, overcast lighting making for a more subtle texture and low-angled, hard sunlight accentuating texture. Either approach can work, and experience will help you decide which type of lighting works best for the look you're after.

There are a few ways you can emphasize surface patterns at the editing stage. The crudest way is to increase the contrast, but these days most photo-editing software has better tools. Try using the Clarity slider and/or the Texture slider, but don't overdo it, as you run the risk of producing a very artificial-looking shot. Also, remember that what works on one part of an image may not look so great on another part, so make local adjustments using gradients or the Brush Tool.

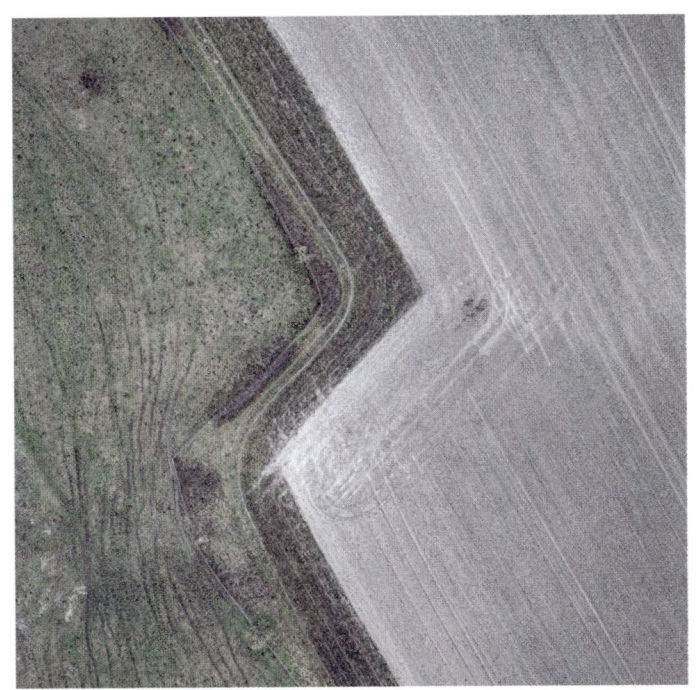

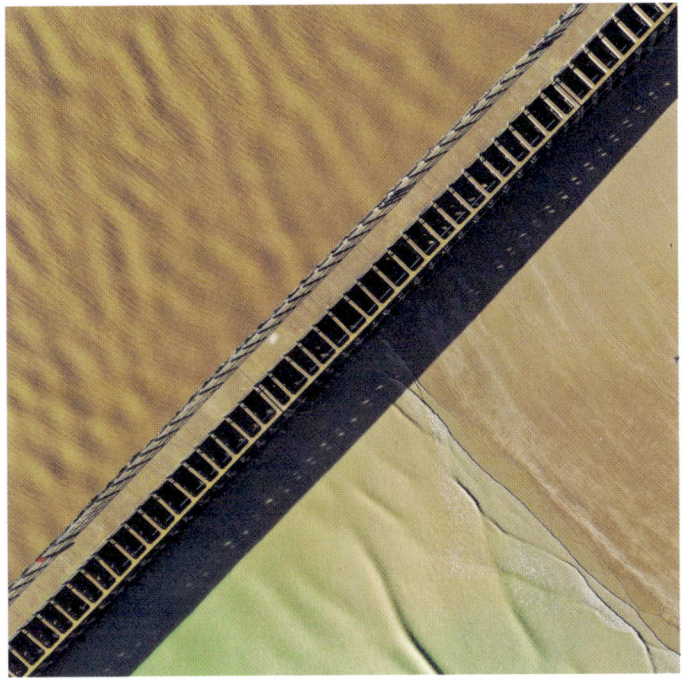

ASSIGNMENT
50

TIPS

- Make use of free weather apps such as Met Office or WeatherPro to predict when you will get partially cloudy conditions.

- Expose for the patches of sunlight to avoid the risk of blowing out highlights. If in doubt, underexpose by 1 or 2 stops using exposure compensation.

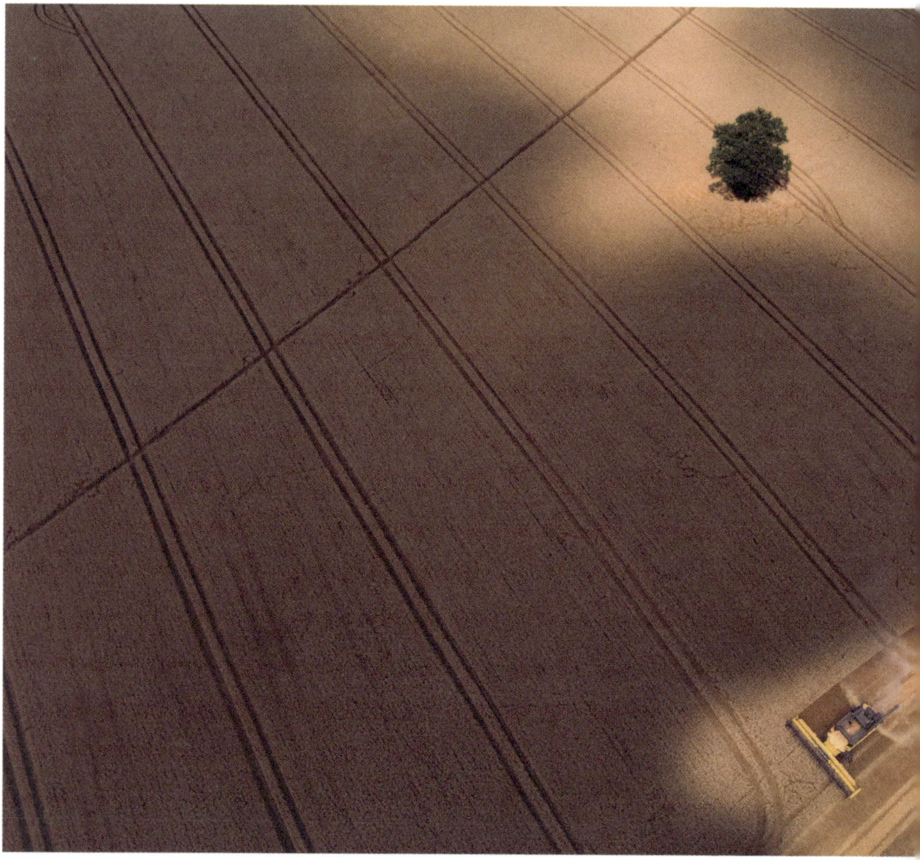

CLOUD SHADOWS

For this assignment, take a drone photo that makes compositional use of the patches of light and dark on a partly cloudy day.

Dappled patches of sunlight and cloud shadows can add a fantastic atmosphere to drone photos. They can also be used to great compositional effect, painting the landscapes with light and dark tones and adding contrast, and this is the basis of your assignment. To achieve dappled light, you need the perfect conditions— summer days that start clear and cloud over as the day progresses are ideal.

It's always a good idea to have a preconceived image in mind and your camera settings dialed in. Then you just need to wait for cloud shadows and patches of sunlight to complement your composition, ideally with your focal point or points illuminated in patches of sunshine.

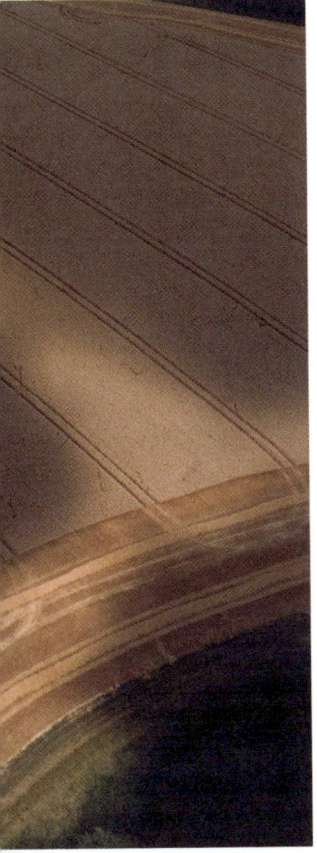

It's important to be aware of wind direction, as from the elevated viewpoint of the drone you will be able to watch the patches of sunlight and clouds moving across the landscape and predict where they will pass through your frame. You will also need a lot of patience (and spare sets of drone batteries) to get the perfect shot. You could even shoot timelapse while you wait and make a short video clip of the cloud shadows moving across the landscape.

◄ I noticed this composition of a tree and combine harvester while shooting video. Within minutes, the clouds had grown, and the sunshine was finished for the day.

ASSIGNMENT

51

TIPS

- If you expose correctly for the brightest parts of the image, the surroundings will be underexposed, which will add contrast and tell the viewer where to look first.

- If you are using natural lighting, timing can be crucial—you may only have seconds to get the shot, so be prepared.

- To get a better feel for the final look of the image, underexpose by a stop or two at the point of capture. You can always do this in the edit, but it often helps to see it live.

LOW-KEY FROM ON HIGH

A low-key image is one that contains mostly darker colors and tones, conveying a sense of drama and mystery. A low-key portrait, for instance, would typically show the subject enveloped in shadow, with the reduced lighting emphasizing only small areas of the frame. For this assignment, you will create a low-key drone image, with the effect achieved with lighting and/or the surroundings themselves.

When the sun is at a very low angle, it will only illuminate certain parts of the landscape, with much of it remaining in deep shadow. If you are shooting at night, your subject may be lit by artificial light but surrounded by an ocean of darkness. Select a subject that is naturally surrounded by darker tones—for instance, dark vegetation, sand, water, or rock—and with a notably lighter tone so that it stands out.

POST-PROCESSING

Process the image to emphasize its darkness. This may mean dropping the overall exposure and/or lowering the exposure in the shadow areas. Don't worry about having large areas of featureless black, as this can draw attention to the main subject.

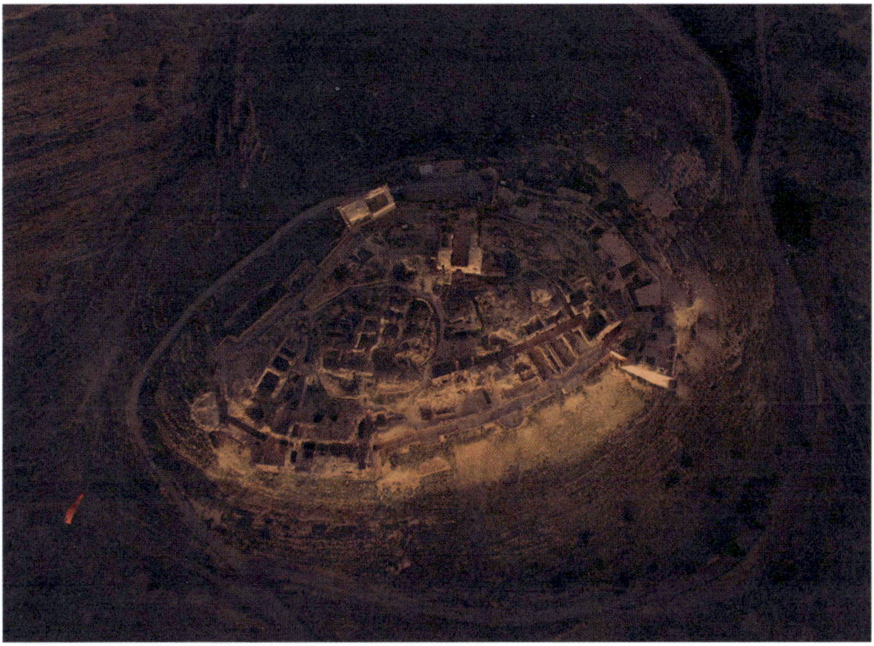

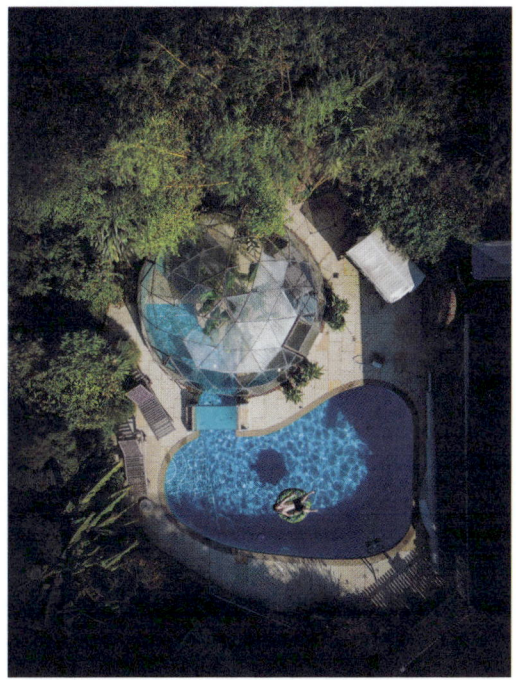

▲ Low evening sun illuminates the ramparts of a Crusader-era fort in Jordan—note the predominantly dark tones.

◄ This swimming pool was surrounded by fairly dark vegetation; adding a vignette enhanced the low-key effect, focusing attention on the main subject.

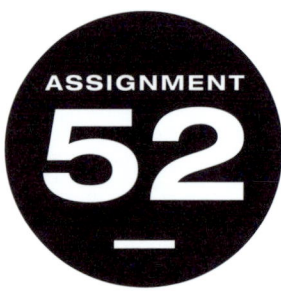

ASSIGNMENT
52

TIPS

- For low-altitude shots, be very careful of splashes and spray, particularly if flying over saltwater. Even if it doesn't bring your drone down, saltwater has a chronic corrosive effect on drones and their cameras.

- Be aware of the maximum operating wind speed of your drone, as this may be exceeded on windy beaches. This info can be found in your drone's manual.

- If you want to freeze the action, select a fast shutter speed (1/500 sec. or faster).

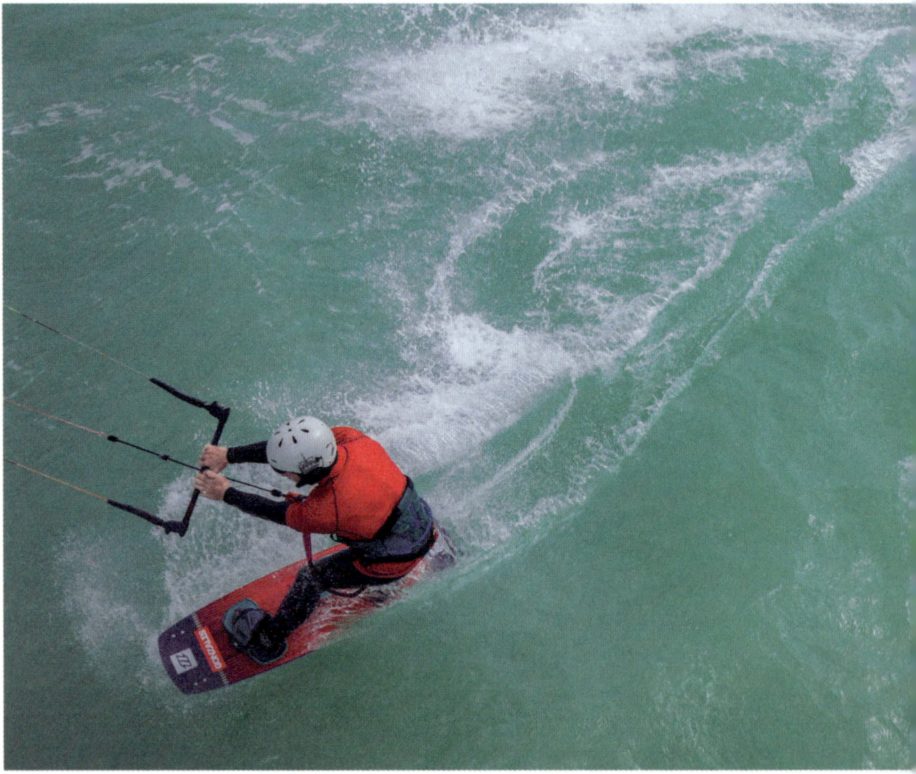

MAKE A SPLASH

Water sports can be an exhilarating spectacle, but if you're stuck on the shore, you may not be able to get the best view of the action. This is where drones come into their own—from above, you'll be able to see every twist, turn, and splash. This assignment is all about capturing an action shot of a water-based sport.

Depending on where you live, you may have access to the ocean, lakes, or rivers where people regularly practice water sports, whether it's dinghy sailing, waterskiing, windsurfing, kitesurfing, or surfing. There are obviously several unique hazards to be aware of when photographing water sports, including strong winds, large waves, salt spray, kite lines, and tall boat masts, so it pays to be very familiar with both your surroundings and your subject matter, particularly if you plan on getting close to the action. Remember that even a gentle collision over water can easily result in the total loss of your drone, so if you have the option, talk to the sportspersons involved before agreeing on a plan.

POST-PROCESSING

When processing the images, adding a touch of clarity and dehaze to areas of spray can enhance the drama. So, get involved and make a splash—just not with your drone!

◀ *A tight shot of a kitesurfer zooming across the waves, achieved using a two-way radio embedded in the kitesurfer's helmet, so I was able to work very closely with him.*

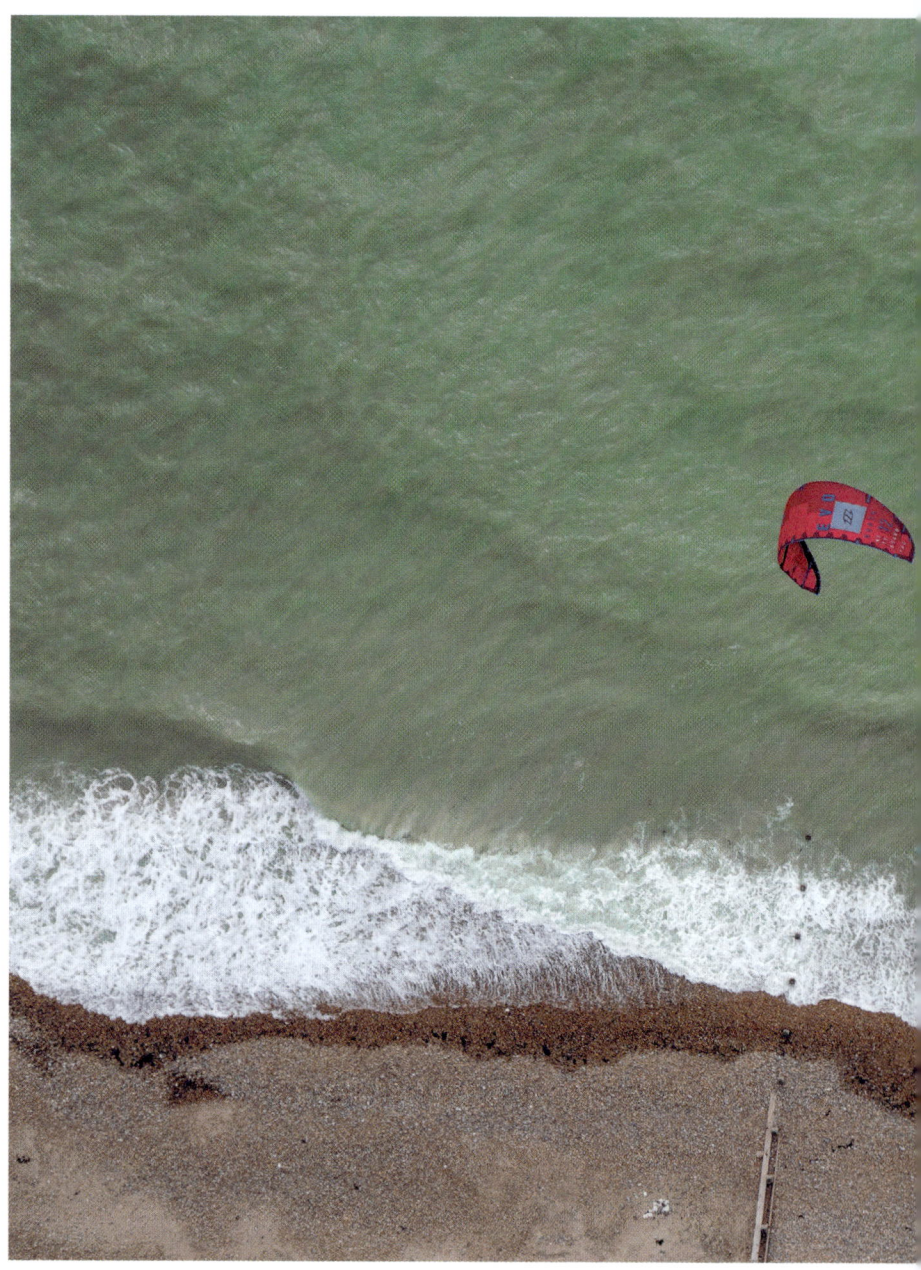

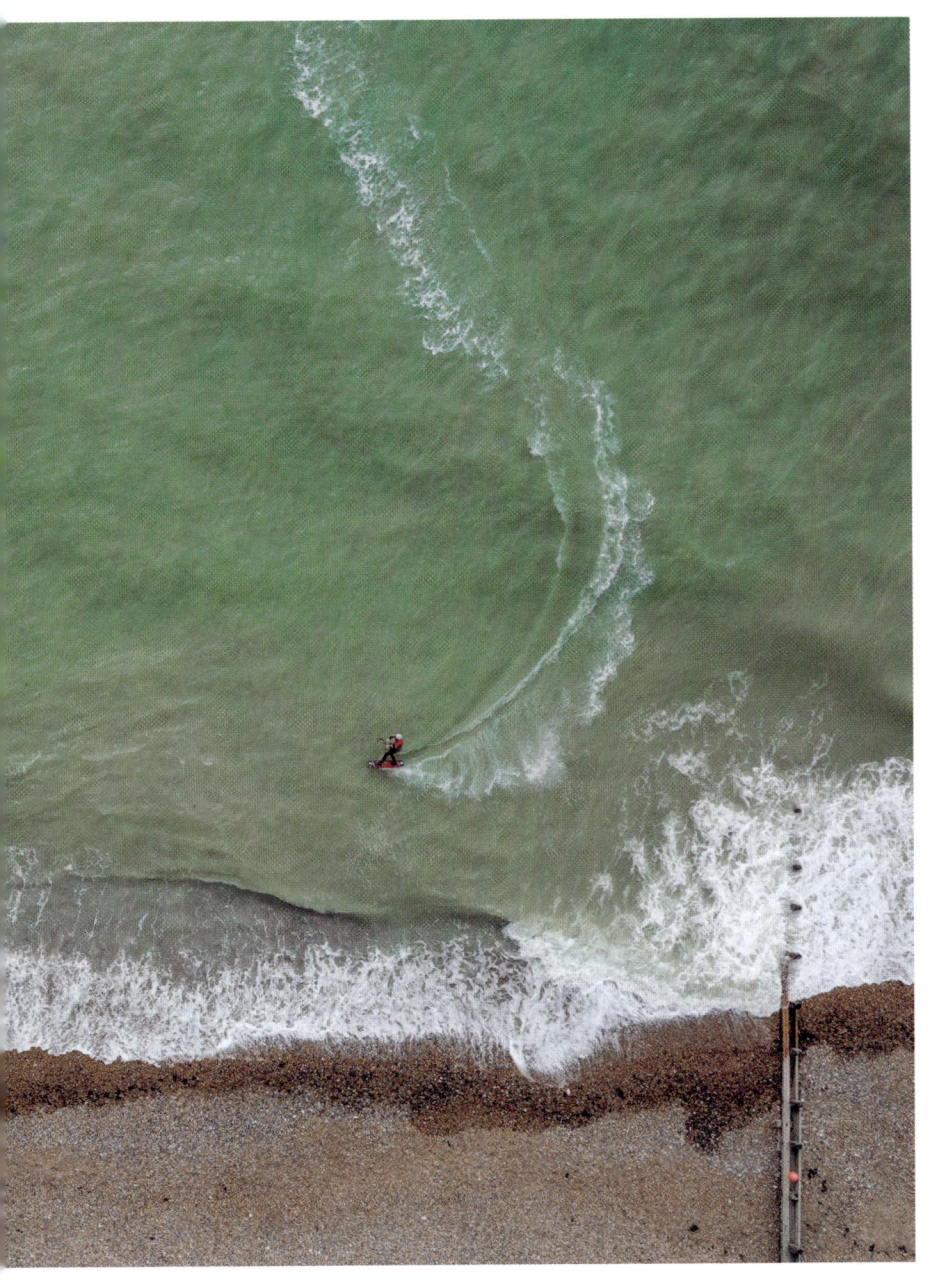

▲ *A graphic top-down shot of the same kitesurfer, with his wake adding nicely to the composition.*

INDEX

First published 2024 by
Ammonite Press
an imprint of Guild of Master Craftsman Publications Ltd
Castle Place, 166 High Street, Lewes, East Sussex, BN7 1XU,
United Kingdom

ISBN 978-1-78145-485-5

Publisher: Jonathan Bailey
Production Director: Jim Bulley
Design Manager: Robin Shields
Senior Project Editor: Tom Kitch
Designer: Ginny Zeal
Editor: Ben Hawkins

Color reproduction by GMC Reprographics
Printed and bound in China

How was the book?
Please post your
feedback and photos:
#52AssignmentsDrone

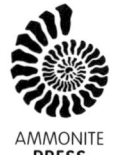

AMMONITE
PRESS

ammonitepress.com

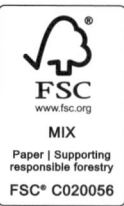

FSC
www.fsc.org
MIX
Paper | Supporting
responsible forestry
FSC® C020056